Praise for From God to DNA

Rem Stokes lays out a brilliant synthesis of our progress as a species from the autocratic and chaos of the past, to an emerging "bottoms up" scientific consensus that God is life itself. His book is personal in an "up close" autobiographical manner yet profound in both historical and scientific insight. This is not another facile statement about faith and science. It is a personal psychological manifesto wrung from struggle and a life well lived. Rem Stokes' thought is shaped by a no nonsense engineering and corporate background. Yet, grace and humility shine from each readable page of his dense prose.

Jack Peltz, Psychologist

In addition to Stokes' breadth of learning -- theologically and historically -- this conversational book is a wonderful and unclouded window into one man's journey of the spirit. It is, also, refreshing to read a critical and yet civil discussion of humanism, when we are beset by thinkers whose sarcasm can speak only to the already skeptical. Enjoyable.

Rev. Hilary Krivchenia, Minister

From God to DNA is a memoir of the author's spiritual journey. This remarkable essay concisely summarizes years of study of religion, history and science. Rem Stokes outlines the logic that led him to reject conventional creedal religions and to embrace the advancements of science as a more compelling way to "answer" life's basic questions. The book is packed with information and insight. You will likely be challenged by this book – in a good way.

Alan Greenland, Optical Design Engineer

In this memoir Rem Stokes promises *A Provocative Journey* and does not disappoint. He amazes me with his gentle persuasive ways. Even the most skeptical will be provoked into examining Rem's well-constructive proofs and conclusions and see whether theirs can withstand the rigor. Particularly revealing to the reader is his contrast of the all too familiar top-down assertion of truth against the truth gleaned by bottom-up approaches through scientific inquiry. You may find his small-g god will comfortably become yours as it has mine.

Dwight Richardson, Retired AT&T Manager

One man's journey to find answers to profound life issues. Whether you agree with the writer's conclusions or not, there is much to ponder. If you have an open, inquiring mind you will enjoy the read.

Joy Simon, RNC

From God to DNA not only shares vignettes of the author's life, and not only sparkles with his obvious warmth, it also provides insight into the development, maturation and architecture of his personal perspective on life's big questions. Those who struggle to make sense of what they experience as a clash between (1) traditional religious teachings with which they were raised and (2) what they have discovered from history and science are likely to discover here, a refreshing breath of fresh air. Whether the author's opinions happen to persuade a particular reader or not, you can trust this book to provoke reflection about issues that matter mightily in the 21st century.

Vid Axel, Writer and Speaker

Rarely do I read something that is so relevant to my life. I have had misgivings with the church theology for most of my many years. It is awkward to discuss one's loss of faith and disbelief in the church. But reading *From God to DNA* was a refreshing breath of fresh air. Rem builds a case that is logical, historical, easy-to-read and supports the many of us who have drifted from conventional religion.

Betty Burns. Inventory Management

Rembert Stokes has written a wonderful book about his spiritual journey from believing in Christianity to being a non-believer. This book will be of great interest to anybody who values reason and the scientific method. It will not be of interest to those who believe in revelation or who think that they have all the answers to the great questions. Overall, I enjoyed reading Stokes' book. It is well written, leaving our confusing philosophical jargon, and can be easily understood by the layperson. It will challenge people of all beliefs.

Raymond Yee, Retired Investment Broker

In *From God to DNA*, author Rem Stokes takes the reader on an informative journey from faith to reason, using his life and his family history as backdrops. In today's world where shouting political pundits and reality TV shows are staples of our culture's daily routine, Stokes' call to a vetting of the important questions in life via science is refreshing. Whatever path you find yourself on in your lives, you will find this text engaging.

Michael Babiarz, Lawyer

This book shows the author's amazing breadth and depth of knowledge, learning and wisdom. It is a useful summary of all the life experiences and learning that has led him away from Christianity to science and a search for better answers. His brilliance shines through this writing and is a wonderful summary of his spiritual development.

Jane Matthews, Author

Rem's intelligent and thoughtful examination of his religious life is, on one hand deeply familiar, and on the other deeply moving. It is thorough, brilliant, and deeply researched, Rem's book combines thousands of years of history with cutting edge scientific research, to present a highly personal journey of faith, discovery, and nearly constant transition. As a student of history, I have trodden many of these same paths, and reached many of the same conclusions. And I have Rem to thank for that. He built churches for many years in support of the Unitarian faith. It was in one of those houses that Rem helped to build that I began my own journey.

Mark Huston, Author

From God to DNA is a quick, thought-provoking journey from theism to atheism through a bevy of sciences. It is readable, enjoyable and accessible. I could feel it and connect to it and learned more about Christianity and the author. Rem provides personal examples and evidence to support his conclusions.

Lawrence Denney, Engineering Manager

Once again, I see what a good writer Rem is for doing his homework, sharing his personal experiences that gives the book its credibility, and meticulously creating a timeline that makes the book so easy to follow even if the concepts are new to you. The subject matter is so compelling. Who knew the expression "Bottoms Up" would have such depth of meaning!

Gaylen Richardson, Councilor

Rem has written an extremely clear and touching account of his life in this memoir. It was interesting to learn how he arrived at his conclusions about "god" and whether indeed "god" exists in this world. We will remember his journey through this controversial subject for a long while. Thank you, Rem.

Mary and Mike McLaughlin, Sales

This book is Rem Stokes' personal journey from religion to free-thinking. He takes you step by step, through his personal transformation, always searching for the truth. I guarantee this journey will cause you to think about what your perception of truth is.

Don Felch, Chemical Engineer

I have had the privilege over several years to share Rem's journey into the historical nature of Christianity. He opened my eyes to the vast volume of information that has been around for centuries that illustrates the many holes in what was given to me as "knowledge" regarding Jesus and the Bible. The discord I felt about religion most of my life is now resolved, and I have great faith in humanity to be able to resolve its problems. We don't need to believe in miracles. We are one. In this book, Rem shows the long bridge between science and spirituality; they truly do belong together.

Ken Sepos, Consultant

Also by Rembert Stokes

Systemic Approach to Problem Solving
Cultivating Generosity: Giving What's Right, Not What's Left

From God to DNA

A Provocative Journey

REM STOKES

LifeRich Publishing books may be ordered through booksellers or by contacting:

LifeRich Publishing
1663 Liberty Drive
Bloomington, IN 47403
www.liferichpublishing.com
1 (888) 238-8637

ISBN: 978-1-4897-0226-5 (sc)
ISBN: 978-1-4897-0227-2 (e)

Printed in the United States of America.

LifeRich Publishing rev. date: 8/4/2014

Dedicated to my Mother

Madge Vincart Stokes

Who was deeply hurt by two churches
but kept her personal faith

Contents

Preface

There is a thread that runs through my life that is much like yours. It is a sacred thread. It weaves through the deep concerns we have with the wonders and mysteries of life. On each of our threads are many beads of different colors, different because we have had unique journeys. On mine, some beads are bright and shining and others are toned down as life tones down with age. The brightest of my beads reflect the enthusiasm I had as a youth while serving as an acolyte in an Episcopal Church. It was so uplifting that I thought about entering the ministry. But something didn't feel right. With time, I acquired many gray beads of doubt, a few black beads of denial, a lot of green beads of excited exploring, thinking and learning and finally a precious blue bead of serene peace. I was drifting from the sacred to the secular and I needed to understand why.

Organized religion – of any denomination or faith – provides a framework into which the human condition is explained and a set of behaviors that promises an ego satisfying continuity of life after death. To doubt these teachings is like gambling with your chances for eternity. If they are truly the instructions of God, as they are presented to be, it is like questioning and rejecting God with the consequences of being rejected by God in return.

So questioning is not only an intellectual exercise but an intensely emotional one. And it proceeds with the tide of cultural opinion and practices going against you. The process of uncoupling is painfully slow. It involves studying the history of ancient times, tracing out the revisionist interpretations, seeing how modern science is undermining those interpretations, questioning your own thoughts and seeking alternative answers that are satisfying and supported by experimental knowledge.

But the whole process, however arduous, only gets you back to ground zero. If successful, it is liberating buts leaves you at the corner of "walk" and "don't walk." Maybe it is somewhat more than neutral. Along the way, one comes to observe the human condition, to learn, and to reach convictions that not only gives one the strength to reject traditional creedal doctrines, but to replace them with more meaningful answers founded in experimental truth. But I get ahead of myself.

With great appreciation, I want to acknowledge those individuals who read the manuscript and gave me helpful suggestions. They include Vid Axel, Michael Babiarz, Betty Burns, Lawrence Denney, Don Felch, Alan Greenland, Mark Huston, Rev. Hilary Krivchenia, Jane Matthew, Mike and Mary McLaughlin, Jack Peltz, Thomas Pool, Gaylen Richardson, Dwight Richardson, Ken Sepos, Joy Simon, and Raymond Yee. I especially want to thank Mark Huston, Alan Greenland, Thomas Pool and Raymond Yee for their detailed reviews and suggestions. With their permission, I have chosen to use their own words as endorsements at the beginning of this book. Thanks to each of you.

In the Beginning, Doubt

My mother was born in Belgium in the little hamlet of Roesburgge-Haringe on January 21, 1902. This was not the family's permanent home because they moved quite often. Her father was a tax collector for alcoholic spirits, and the government required him to move about every three years lest he become too friendly with any of the tavern owners. Even so, he was seen "measuring the sidewalk" many nights on his way home from work. The family eventually settled in Poperinge, a neighboring town to Ypres, the famous cloth center of Flanders, and shortly the scene of the heaviest and most sustained fighting in WWI.

My father was born in Lynchburg, South Carolina on January 10, 1898. Lynchburg was a farming town with only a few stores on each side of the railroad tracks. My paternal grandfather owned one of those stores. It was a general-purpose store with food, ice and farm supplies. Outside the store was a sawmill that he operated and a coal yard from which he sold and delivered coal. In addition, he had time to raise 12 children and take care of a blind aunt.

To accommodate the express trains, the local trains would pull off on the sidings and wait for the express trains to pass. During the wait, the engineers would frequently get off the train and go into my grandfather's store for conversation and an occasional purchase. I bring this up because one of the engineers was named Mr. Ryan, and my grandfather apparently liked him a lot. With 12 children, Grandpa must have run out of names because he gave my father the middle name of Ryan. My father's first name was Rembert, his mother's family name. And that is how I acquired my name as a junior.

When the United States got involved in World War I, my father was already in the National Guard and was a natural candidate to serve overseas. Training took place at Camp Sevier near Greenville, South Carolina. He was assigned to be the company's bugler and found it to be an off-and-on job with gaps of time between scheduled calls. So like his father, he opened a canteen to provide miscellaneous items for the troops, not the least of which was refreshing multi-flavored Italian ice. While in training, he met some of the local families, and especially the Griffin family who befriended him and offered to help with employment after the war. He never forgot.

The Americans actually entered the war very late. Dad arrived in France in late May of 1918. Armistice was signed on November 11, 1918.

Upon arrival, his unit was trained in France and moved to Belgium – to Poperinge to be specific. He was in the area for only two months, just long enough to get gassed and attract the sympathy of a young girl who would become his future wife. By all rights, I should have been born a little Brussels sprout, but the Great War intervened and, lucky me, I was born American.

Dad continued to bugle and run his canteen for the troops. One day while relaxing in the Talbot House in Poperinge, a military R & R center, he noticed a young girl entering a photography shop across the street. She was wearing a lovely white dress – probably the only nice dress she had after three years of war – to have her picture taken. The occasion was her 16th birthday and the picture was to be a present for her father. My father-to-be couldn't resist following her into the shop and trying to start a conversation. With no luck! She knew English. All Belgium children are required to take four years of English in school. But most Belgium parents had warmed their daughters not to "pick up" with any soldiers. It would come to no good when the war was finally over.

Not to be outdone, my father tried time and again to get her to speak to him. Still no luck! Then my father, who had a rather short temper, probably said something like this: "Fine thing. We come over here to fight a war for you and you won't even say hello." Still nothing. Nothing! So my father left disappointed. Or, as they say in Lynchburg, with his tail between his legs.

But revenge is sweet. The next week he returned to the photographer and bribed him with goodies from his canteen for a wallet-sized picture of the still nameless girl.

Shortly afterwards, his unit was ordered to the front line. In the military tactics of WWI, the bugler had a second job as point man. He was to go into no-man's-land first, assure it was safe, and signal his troops to advance.

On one particular occasion, it didn't work out so well for dad. He was badly gassed and rendered unconscious. Either the Germans anticipated the attack and sprayed mustard gas or the Americans were using gas and had a tragic wind shift. We could never find out. When his unit finally advanced, they recognized him, thought him to be dead and had the government issue a death certificate to his family. The British followed up, removing the bodies and taking them back to military medical tents.

As it happened – truer than fiction – the same 16-year-old girl was serving as a candy-striper, helping out as a volunteer to relieve the medics for more urgent needs. Her job was to establish the identity of the bodies and dispatch them to the proper medical units based on country and organization. While going through my father's wallet, she found her own picture. Can you imagine what must have gone through her mind? Oh my God; this is the soldier I refused to speak to!

Needless to say, he recovered and they finally had that first conversation. Over the following weeks and months, they saw each other as the war permitted. This is the stuff that romance is made of. And in a reasonably short time, a relationship was turning into love.

The town of Poperinge was within shelling distance of Mount Kemmel that the Germans occupied. Many residents moved out of direct danger by erecting a tent city in the farmland. My mother-to-be named their tent "Chateau Magdalena" which was her first name. She invited my father to meet her parents and he befriended them with "luxury" food items from his canteen that were otherwise almost impossible to get.

I think you should know that my father loved to bargain. He would take canned bacon, Spam and other military rations into the countryside and trade them for fresh eggs, fruits and vegetables. The farmers loved the rare treats they couldn't buy and my father loved to carry fresh food back to the troops.

On one occasion, General Blackjack Pershing visited dad's encampment and asked to visit the mess hall. He observed the fresh foods that were not military rations and asked the mess sergeant where they came from. The mess sergeant told him and General Pershing asked for my father to report to his tent. My father instantly thought he was going to be reprimanded or given a dishonorable discharge. Instead, the General thanked him and gave him a pass that entitled him to ride on any military conveyance to continue his bargain hunting. Dad used it to advantage for bargaining, but also courting, the two being pretty much the same thing actually.

When the war ended, my father promised to marry the young Miss Magdalena Vincart and bring her to America. He sailed home in mid-March 1919 with a plan to return. Her parents warned her not to put too much faith in it. But the couple wrote regularly and kept the relationship alive. After discharge, my father worked till December to save enough money to book return passage for the two of them. Then he signed on as a laborer on a banana boat going to Europe to get free passage for himself.

The plan was for him to arrive in time for Christmas 1919. But the banana boat broke down and there was no way to inform her. Christmas came and went and Magdalena was emotionally crushed. It didn't help that her parents warned her of this possibility. Finally, one week late, he arrived and explained what happened. The explanation was not important. What was important was that he had arrived.

Now the subject turned to marriage. Belgium was essentially a Catholic nation and my maternal grandparents were not only Catholic, they were pillars of the church. When the couple went to the church for arrangements, the Catholic priest asked my father-to-be if he planned to raise his children as Catholics. My father said no, absolutely not! The town of Lynchburg was essentially Southern

Baptist. All of his relatives and friends were Baptists and he would want his children to be part of the family. Well! The Catholic Church refused to marry them to the great disappointment of my Belgium relatives and especially my mother-to-be.. Instead they were married on the steps of the town hall by the local burggermaster (mayor) on January 14, 1920.

So my dear mother had just experienced her first disappointment with institutional religion, a blow she would not forget. In baseball terms, it would be strike one for my mother with more to come. It seems to me that when a church puts a practice before the supreme human value of love, it distorts the most fundamental principles of life. It has certainly made me lose some respect of the institutional church. I have always believed that you should love people and use things, not that you should love things and use people.

When my parents arrived in the United States, they finally settled in Greenville, South Carolina. Greenville is located in the northwestern part of South Carolina, in the Piedmont region (foot of the mountain), cradled next to Paris Mountain.

Greenville started its serious development in 1815 when an entrepreneur named Vardry McBee bought somewhat over 11,000 acres, began selling real estate and bringing business to the village. It was originally called Pleasantburg. But as the village grew into a town, the name was changed to Greenville, named after the lush green trees.

One of the things McBee did that I found very interesting was he gave land to each religious denomination on which to build its church. He felt churches made the town socially stable. He was probably right, but he may have over done it. As a child I was impressed with how many churches there were and they were all Christian.

Closer to my childhood, I remember two streets named after him. McBee Street was second only to Washington Street in prominence and dead-ended exactly in front of the Junior High School. Vardry Street was less imposing but was the address of the Senior High School. I travelled these streets many times without knowing the history behind them.

At that time, Greenville was the textile center of the South. Textile mills surrounded the downtown with their quaint mill villages and mill-end stores. The textile industry grew up there for several reasons. First, there was a modest river that flowed through town called Reedy River. It had some significant shoals that allowed the earliest cotton mills to power the plants with waterwheels before they had electricity. The second reason was because the water was so pure it did not require the extra expense of filtering. The water originated in the Appalachian Mountains and filtered down hill through miles of granite before it got to Greenville.

I mention this because the mills were a source of summer employment. Working in a cotton mill for just one summer was enough to convince me I wanted nothing to do with it. When I graduated from high school, the ceremony was held, where else, in Textile Hall, the largest auditorium in town.

My father was in the photo-engraving business initially, but had to give it up because the acid fumes were bad on his weakened lungs from having been gassed in WWI. Then he went into the wholesale produce business. And that lasted until the Great Depression hit and the average person couldn't afford luxury foods. The businesses that held up reasonably well were inexpensive things like fishing hooks, playing cards and beer to soften the misery. That's when my father went into the liquor business.

Well, as I mentioned earlier, Dad was a Southern Baptist. And my Mother had amicably converted. My parents attended church and I went to Sunday School and earned a chest full of medals for good attendance. What I learned there was the traditional young person's exposure to Christian doctrine. I was told that God created the world and was infinitely good, knowledgeable and powerful. He had a son, Jesus, who was meek, good, did miracles and ultimately died on the cross to save us from our sins. After three days He rose from the dead and ascended into Heaven. We are to believe in Jesus by faith, not good works like Jesus did. Ultimately Jesus will return to earth for a final judgment. Those who believe in Him will go to Heaven; those who don't will go to Hell. So ended the lesson.

I had trouble with this from the start. My issues were young boy practical issues like "Who created God to begin with?"; "Where did He live?"; "What material did He use?"; What was time before time started?"; "Where was space before He made space?"; "Where is Heaven and Hell?"; "How could God have a Son if he didn't have a wife? When I asked my simple questions I was told I was too young to understand. When I repeated the questions, I was told: Because I said so!

My parents even signed me up for Summer Bible School in the American Legion Lodge, my father, of course, being a member of the American Legion. What I remember most was how hot it was in the lodge during the summer before air-conditioning. Worst, the lodge was next door to McPherson Park where I would much rather be playing. It was my favorite place. If I was not at home, you could generally find me at McPherson Park.

The Baptist church had a reputation of watching which way the federal flag was flying and lining up with it for political reasons. My father's entry into the liquor business was at the tail end of Prohibition and the close association was too much for the Baptist reputation. After a decade of loyal membership in the church, our family was asked out. OUT! This didn't hurt the business because the same Baptist parishioners still bought from my Dad, but he had to deliver to their back doors.

But it was too much for my Mother. This was strike two by an institutional church. And she refused to go back to the plate, fearing striking out. For one church to interfere with honest love in marriage and another church to interfere with honest work in business was much too much for her. She felt that individual leaders in churches were imposing their wishes on the lives of others. There will always be a "Grand Green Dragon" who wants to lord it over others. So she kept a safe distance.

She was the most moral, loving person I have ever known. As a child I wondered how she separated her goodness and morality from the institutional church, when the churches were supposed to be the champions and guardians of love and morality. Now I know her morality was an innate quality in the human breast, not a gift from the church, and her loving nature was a living reflection of how she was raised as a child.

Cut apart from church life, my parents let my older sister, Vivian, and me decide where or whether we wanted to attend church. For a child, that was not a hard decision. Our peer groups were attending churches. My sister was dating a Presbyterian boy and she easily drifted to that denomination. Being younger by five years, my interests were in sports. At that time, the town had a Sunday School Basketball League. Most of my friends were Episcopalians and they needed another player. And with essentially no theological thought, I became a guard on the Episcopalian team. So both my sister and I found our niches quite easily, but superficially I'm afraid.

Only my niche became more than basketball. I was at that impressionable age where I needed some kind of affirmation beyond by parents and friends. And the Episcopalian church had a plan to accommodate it. They permitted young boys to serve as acolytes and actually participate in the services. I loved it. It seemed so uplifting, so regal, so god-like. I threw myself into it with all my might, arriving at church early, shaping the candle-wicks, polishing the cross, laying out the cassocks and cottas and waiting for the service. I was thrilled to lead the procession, carrying the cross held high, lighting the candles, kneeling at the altar, being unnaturally solemn for a teenager, and reversing the process at the end of the service. I was in seventh heaven. I thought to myself that the church couldn't function without me.

But like most dreams, this one had to end. There was also a rational part of me that began thinking about the words we were saying and the doctrine it implied. There came a time when I starting mumbling during passages I doubted. I just couldn't bring myself to say things I was questioning. At that age I didn't know what was right, but I knew I was uncomfortable. And the mumbling increased Sunday after Sunday.

I don't think that my questioning of the theology of the church had anything to do with the horrific experiences my parents had with the practices of two churches. There comes a time in a child's life when he asks more sophisticated questions and expects to get reasonable answers from the adults in his life. The so-called answers I was getting were not reasonable. In fact, they defied reason altogether.

So many people accepted on faith that God created the world and sent his only son Jesus to save us from original sin. My problem was that the church formulated the doctrine of Original Sin in the first place and then offered the only way to be saved from it. That sounded like circular thinking to me, even as a child.

People around me believed in angels, the efficacy of prayer, the need for forgiveness, and a final judgment with the promise of heaven or the damnation of hell. Everywhere around me I heard the continuous drumbeat of supernaturalism. Do people really believe this or do they want to be affiliated with symbolic goodness. Don't any adults share my doubts?

I was not alone in this dilemma. Many of my friends were asking the same questions and getting the same non-answers. We would spend endless hours talking about theological and philosophical issues that troubled us with no resolution except what seemed inconsistent with everything we were being taught in school about how to think for ourselves. It was particularly troubling that all the adults I respected, my aunts, uncles and parents of my friends, went to church and seemed to take it seriously, except in their everyday practices toward the colored people. To this day, I do not know whether church-going was a sign of faith or just respectability. Maybe both.

In school I was reasonably good in math, physics and mechanical drawing. It seemed appropriate to enter Clemson College (now University) and enroll in mechanical engineering. This was an all-important experience in my life. It was a true turning point. My professors insisted that engineering was a life-and-limb profession. The products we designed impacted the lives of people in a very tangible way. We were instructed to calculate our answers to four decimal points and then add a big safety factor. There was absolutely no room for hunches, guesses, beliefs or intuition. "Just the facts, ma'am."

At the same time I was attending the Clemson Episcopalian Church where there was a very likable priest with whom I could easily relate. When I brought up my problem with reason versus faith, he was very helpful. He said that much of the church doctrine could not be put to the test of reason and has to be taken on faith.

I knew I was entering a career in engineering that would be my bread and butter. I further knew I could not live with a compartmentalized mind, being rational at work and faithful at church. About the same time I heard Emerson's quote: "Nothing is ultimately sacred except the integrity of your own mind." That did it. That was the tipping point for me. And that is when I left the Christian Church.

Intellectually, I walked away from Christianity. But for many years I knew I had not left it emotionally.

My first job was at the distinguished Bell Telephone Laboratories. I couldn't have been happier. BTL was at the cutting-edge of communication technology. It is said they held a record for obtaining two patents a day since 1925. Including some extremely important ones like the transistor, zone-refining and solar batteries. They required all new employees to continue their education by providing a three-year, Master of Science level program, in the disciplines affecting their work. I was out of my league for most of the electrical engineering, but managed to survive. It was here that I was introduced to new technologies like statistics, Boolean algebra, crystallography, etc. The deeper I got into understanding the principles of nature, the further I got away from thinking about anything supernatural.

My initial Bell Labs location was in Summit, New Jersey and it was there that I found the Unitarian Universalist Church. It is a church with no creed. The spiritual goal was to search for truth. Doubt was welcomed, even encouraged, since doubt is the friend of truth. I knew I was at home. Each of the members was on a different religious path in approaching that goal. So we humorously said: "We agree to disagree without being disagreeable."

I was with Bell Labs for 25 years. My group developed station sets, the devices that are better known as telephones or more simply phones. Is anybody old enough to remember station-to-station calls? I worked on card-dialing phones, self-dialing phones, automatic-dialing phones, conference phones, speaker-phones, public coin telephones, Picturephones, radio phones and finally High Capacity Mobile Telephones that are now familiarly called cell phones. During this exciting design phase, I was awarded 22 patents.

In 1962, I was transferred to the Indianapolis Bell Labs and given supervisory responsibility for developing the new, single-slot coin telephone for the Bell System. While working on coin telephones, the government recognized the need to replace the silver coinage with a low cost substitute. The reason for the change is obvious in hindsight. When the cost of the raw material exceeds the face value of a coin, people will melt down the coinage and sell the raw material. I am told that Mexico has lost eleven gold coins for this reason.

Well, I invented the laminated coinage that would replace silver coins. The U.S. Treasury and Congress adopted this design in 1964 and it has been in usage since then. Our timing was good. Starting in 1971, the Hunt brothers of Texas starting cornering the market for silver and drove the price from about two dollars to 51 dollars an ounce. We chose not to patent the design but to give all rights to the government. Many foreign countries now use this design for the same reason.

While in Indianapolis I attended All Souls Unitarian Church and it was there that I met Lee Skeeters. Lee was raised in the Baptist Church as I was, but became more liberal while studying for her undergraduate degree at the University of Illinois. After graduation, she was employed by Eli Lilly Pharmaceutical Company that was located in Indianapolis. It was there that fellow employers told her they were attending an evening study group on the Great Books and invited her to attend. It was held in the All Souls Unitarian Church. She attended and came to know the minister, a few friends, and sample the theology. That is when she joined the church. Later, she went on to earn a masters degree in social work and was employed by the Indianapolis Public Schools.

Lee and I were single, middle-aged, employed and home owners when we met. From the start we shared many things in common. Both were Unitarian and shared common beliefs and values. Both of us loved books and she manned the used book table during coffee hour after church services. Slowly I became her best customer and found myself buying books I already owned just to hang around the book table with her. Well it didn't take long before we started dating. Then I realized I had met a gem. She was the most gracious person I had ever met and was always concerned for others. She was also a beautiful, well-dressed lady. How could this not lead to love? Within a year or so, we decided to get married. So she resigned her job as a social worker with the public schools and took on a case load of one: me.

At exactly the same time in 1966, Bell Labs asked me to move back to Holmdel, New Jersey and supervise the mechanical development of the Picturephone. So Lee and I sold our homes, drove to New Jersey, bought a new home and finally got married in my first Unitarian Church in Summit. It started as a happy marriage and has remained so for 47 years. Lee and I had our separate interests that gave us the freedom to be our individual selves, but we also had many common activities and friends that made a rich life. Of all the good things that have happened to me, marrying Lee is the best.

And yes, we found the closest Unitarian Church in Lincroft and started attending. There we met four other couples that became our dearest friends: the Forrests, Richardsons, Porters and Moissons. We partied together, sailed together and vacationed together. On New Years Eve, we would gather at one of our homes and leave the streets to the heavy drinkers. We cherished those friendships and stay in touch to this day.

Lee was very aware that I was losing my allegiance to anything mystical. She listened patiently to my ramblings and supported me in the quest for rational answers. As a loving mate, she was very present in helping me clarify my thoughts. But I want it clearly understood that these are my conclusions and mine alone.

I would have happily stayed at Bell Labs until retirement, but the government intervened. The Justice Department divested the

Bell System in an effort to offer the public more product and service options. Overnight, the scientific flavor of the Labs was changed to a marketing orientation to compete in the new open market. For me, this was a sad day. The technological edge was blunted. Many of my co-workers left for other jobs.

Just then, serendipity happened. I got a call from my former Bell Labs boss, Claude Davis, who had moved to Motorola a few years before and encouraged me to join him. It was a bittersweet moment for me. I loved and respected the old Labs, but I knew things had changed. And I sort of feared starting with a new company at age 48 and rebuilding my reputation. Worse, it involved moving my family, leaving our church, doctors, barber, convenient shopping, and especially our close and dear friends.

We did move to Motorola at Schaumburg, Illinois in 1978. There we became corporate gypsies. Motorola really didn't have a job for me. At my age, I was paid too much to simply design products, my first love. So they used me as a general problem solver and moved us wherever they thought I could make a contribution. This included one year at Schaumburg, four years at Ft. Lauderdale, Florida, four years at Austin, Texas, back to Schaumburg and finally to Buffalo Grove, Illinois. My wife, Lee, thought that they were letting us try out possible retirement areas. And we always found Unitarian Churches in each of these places.

Our last move was back to Schaumburg in 1985. We bought a home in Inverness and lived there 25 years, many of which were after my retirement in 1994. Finally the American dream of home ownership began to fade, as did our health, and we moved into The Garlands of Barrington, a wonderful retirement home where we are today.

When Oliver Wendell Holmes was asked why he went to church he replied: "I have a spiritual plant in me that needs to be watered." I feel the same way. I need a church that is high in morality, high in intellectual content, high in questioning, high is acceptance, high in seeking the truth, but low in doctrine, pretending to have the answers.

The Unitarian-Universalist Church became very meaningful to me. I took on the unwanted job of fund-raising, and through my life I have helped 77 churches. And as we moved from one Motorola facility to another, we found the local Unitarian–Universalist Churches had inadequate facilities and I became deeply involved in building six churches.

During the latter years with Motorola, the concept of six-sigma quality was popularized. I became quite proficient in this subject and taught courses in quality and the design of experiments at Motorola University. I also wrote a book entitled *Systematic Approach to Problem Solving* for Motorola, converted it into a course and taught it for many semesters. In retirement, I formed a company and consulted with local businesses for about six years on the subject of incorporating quality practices into their operations.

During this technical career, I continued to have unresolved questions about the doctrines of the church. I wanted to say it was all mythology and declare myself an agnostic, atheist or humanist. But I couldn't rationally do that. I had no convincing arguments to support the non-belief position and would have to take it on faith, the very problem I had with accepting church doctrine. I can only say it felt more rational and comfortable, but there was no "proof text" to support it. So I continued to worry and question and wonder if I was wrong and what the cosmic consequences would be.

It was not until retirement that I had the time to read and really focus on the evolution of the Christian church and religion in general. Up until that time, my attention had been primarily directed to the literature in my career and I felt very well versed in fields of engineering and science. Now was the opportunity to expand my horizon and possibly my knowledge. So I started reading psychology, philosophy, and history.

I particularly enjoyed reading Will Durant's multi-volume History of Western Civilization. It filled in so many gaps that I was never told about in my early years. And now I know why.

This is a good place to share with you some of my findings and conclusions.

Part I

Reflecting on the Past

Thinking About God

The word God is unquestionably the most revered word in the English language. Millions upon millions of believers hold the concept behind the word God in awe. For them it is the answer to the most difficult questions and the lifeline for their most personal hopes.

Since the beginning, mankind has been aware of the vastness and mystery of the universe as well as the fearfulness and difficulty of surviving in it. Our ancestors came into immediate contact with the elements in a way we can scarcely imagine. For early mankind especially, the search for answers was more than philosophical. There was a sense of urgency about it. Unquestionably, fear was a dominant emotion of the human condition. Early man, trying to cope with the uncertainty and potential dangers in life, looked for explanations. And the explanations he found could only be expressed in a mystical way, perhaps with touches of awe and reverence and above all, wonder.

For many cultures, the explanation they found was god or many gods. What is common to all the gods is that they afford their cultures the assurances that life has meaning, structure and promise. Whether or not they can fulfill these promises is another thing. What is important is people have hope and belief.

The shorthand for this all-embracing explanation is god, spelled with a small "g," and reasonably defined as the repository of all unanswered questions and answered desires.

In my opinion, there is nothing wrong with having a shorthand name as a convenient way to express the enormity of the unknown that surrounds us from birth to death. And because of the enormity of this unknown, I, too, hold it in awe and wonder.

For me, it is interesting to speculate how the concept of god arose.

I'm not sure that anyone knows, but I am sure it did many times. So there should be a trail of evidence, so to speak, and an emerging pattern that we could trace.

What follows is a personal trip for me. I have no wish to disturb anyone's belief in his or her god. And I would be saddened if I accidently knocked the props out from under anyone who deeply needs his faith.

Neither am I limiting this discussion to the Christian God. I am talking about all gods that are worshipped and revered everywhere – past and present. It is the same emotional feeling in all people that seems to yearn for a god. With this disclaimer, let's go exploring.

What comes to mind for me first is when our distant ancestors had relatives die, they often encountered them in their dreams in a way that seemed very real. I have the same surreal feelings when I see my parents and friends in dreams. For primitive man, it was natural to wonder if they were still alive in another form and visiting from a different space. The idea of an alternate existence in a new dimension was enticing, comforting and maybe possible.

We have also learned that morality came long before gods or religions. You can see moral behavior in animals that certainly don't have either religions or gods. And you can see the essence of the same moral values in all people regardless of culture or their local religions.

It is beyond question that early society created rules of conduct to regulate and comfort them. Even animals in groups are known to make and enforce rules of conduct.

For me, the final piece of the puzzle was that early tribal life was very aware of the alpha male concept. Among the apes there is a dominant male who exercises power and control over the other males. Since there were always tribal members who broke the rules out of self-interest, I can imagine the tribe wondering if it wouldn't be advantageous to have a powerful male figure that would enforce the rules and help regulate life?

With these and similar ancestral realities, it is a short jump to connect the dots and have early man yearn for an invisible alpha male in alternate space to enforce morality by fear and guilt.

Excuse me for this over-simplistic explanation of the evolution of the god concept. No one really knows for sure. And neither do I. But I am convinced the arc of development followed the common fears and emotional needs of the human race under conditions of uncertainty.

But there is more. Here is where culture enters the picture. Cultures dress their alpha male enforcers.

Beyond control, cultures have an insatiable need for answers. And since the "alpha male enforcer" doesn't talk, the culture puts words in his mouth. They attributed to him their highest values and provoked from him the answers they needed to have by way of myths and big story explanations like creation. Now he is more than an "alpha male enforcer," he is a god. And all cultures created their own in the likeness of their values. To be believable and retain the assigned roles, these gods had to be worshipped to keep the illusion alive. And the belief must be carefully taught and passed down from generation to generation.

And all the people who relate to this new god form a religion. Because of the enormous uncertainty in life, religions fill a real need in the psyche of the human race. If people aren't born into a religion, they will create one. And if they are born into a religion that doesn't suit them, they will move to a new religion that does. The need is internal to each of us and the god concept satisfies that inner need.

But all gods and all religions are created by man for man's own comfort. God is a creative concept, but it is only a concept of our own making. To call something god when you have no knowledge of what it means is a frightening thing.

Most of the faithful will argue if God is only a concept, who created the world? It is so natural to think of everything having a beginning and an end. But in reality, only organic things have a birth and death. We impose this cookie cutter concept on everything. Surely the world had a beginning and will have an end. But an inorganic thing like a rock has no birth and no death. A chunk of granite may weather or erode or get crushed, but it continues to be granite in different forms. And while it defies our intuition, the world is not organic and the concept of beginning and ending has no known meaning.

I find it fascinating how the human can conceive of an idea, forget that he conceived it, and then worship it. This requires an intense need to believe in something other than self. Or it exposes wants one cannot provide for him or her self.

Other cultures dressed their gods differently. The Greeks surrounded themselves with hundreds of pagan gods who rewarded prayers with favors. People worshiped them to receive immediate benefits, not future benefits. They prayed for rain for the crops, for their daughter's fertility, for victory in war, and for relief from disasters. There were many gods thought capable of delivering different benefits and delivering them now.

Christianity gained acceptance in the Roman Empire through such a pagan prayer for favors rendered NOW. Emperor Constantine bargained in pagan fashion that if Christ would help him win the Battle of Milvian Bridge now, he would declare Christianity as the religion of the Roman Empire. He won the battle in 312 C.E. and lived up to his promise. Christianity became the religion of the Roman Empire as defined by the Nicene Creed in 325 C.E.

From a pagan god perspective, I wonder why the Greeks did not pray for a future benefit like life after death. Later religions would change that.

The early Jewish tribes had separate gods. It was not until they were captured by the Babylonians in 586 B.C.E. that they were exposed to the religion of Zoroaster. Zoroaster, a Persian prophet, believed there was only one god and preached a religion of dualism including opposites like good and evil, and heaven and hell. In 550 B.C.E., Cyrus of Persia crushed Babylon and encouraged the Jews to go home. The Jews were so pleased they named Cyrus a messiah and adopted the idea of monotheism.

The strange part of the story for me is that former Jewish gods like El and Baal that were once revered and worshiped simply faded from history. But so did the early gods of the Incas and Aztecs. To paraphrase General Douglas MacArthur, old gods don't die, they just fade away. This could only happen if gods are simply in the minds of men.

The problem comes when god with a small-g is elevated to God with a capital-G. God with a capital-G is no longer just a shorthand way of referring to the endless mystery. Capital-G God is conceived in the minds of humanity in certain cultures as a tangible, personalized God with human qualities and above all, power. These are the powers to create or destroy, to bless or condemn, to intervene or ignore, to favor goodness over evil: all powers that we attribute to a capital-G God.

Our need for acceptance now extends to this capital-G God, even though our ancestors in every culture created their own unique God or Gods. If we ever needed to be accepted, and if this God were real, we certainly would need to be accepted by our local God. I remember the Christian God of my youth was characterized as an all powerful, judgmental entity who was an anthropomorphic being with white hair, beard and all. And even though it is a product of our own minds, it was considered wiser to relate to it respectfully... just in case.

Each society commandeers Capital-G God for its own. Christians believe the "true" God is theirs. We ascribe our social values to this God and elevate them to commandments, the observance of which is thought to have life or death consequences.

For me, it is a big jump from the looseness of multiple pagan gods providing benefits to the tightness of structured creedal religions requiring belief. Somewhere these many gods had to be forgotten and replaced by one monotheistic god. And that one god had to be both controller and provider. So next, God had to be assigned an encyclopedic list of powers and behaviors. This is obviously the doings of human hopes and fears. Who else but we could do it? As someone wisely said, gods are made in the image of man, not man in the image of god. The only way to get traction with a particular concept of god is to surround it with noble values and repeat it endlessly.

No one has ever seen a god, not even Moses who allegedly saw only a burning bush. No one can define any of his properties or attributes except the ones handed down by our culture. Out of the great population of believers, no one can characterize God, whether physical or pure energy. If our lives depended on it, we could not honestly tell you anything about God, except what our culture has taught us to believe. And to my knowledge, there are no proof texts of the existence of any god known to scholars. So God remains an undefined proposition that we desperately want to believe in as a basis of hope, morality and reward. He exists to the degree we believe in Him.

Calling something a god is a kind of answer that doesn't answer anything at all. To name is not to know. It is not even a meaningful word if it cannot be defined. The dictionary definition of god starts with the words "a being conceived" and then lists only attributes, not properties. When I speak to any two people who profess to believe in the same god, I have no assurance they are indeed talking about the same god. In a humorous way God can be thought of as an invisible cafeteria of noble pseudo-answers from which people can pick and choose to feed their individual emotional hungers.

All of the religions that came out of Asia Minor, known for their warring tribes -- Judaism, Christianity and Islam -- evoked a God of power who would ultimately judge the transgressions of immoral behavior. But you don't need a God to have a religion. Neither the Confucian nor Buddhist religions have a God. Such religions are generally practiced in the Far East that is known for putting the community before the individual and depends on revered social customs to provide orderly conduct. It is strange for Westerners to think of a religion without a God. But a large part of the population of the world does just that.

To my satisfaction, I have come to understand and appreciate the role of spiritual mysticism in the lives of my ancestors seeking answers to life-confronting questions in a pre-scientific era. And I am sensitive to the continuing needs of all people who live with uncertainty in a world without answers. But as time has passed, accumulated knowledge has eroded many of the cherished beliefs we hold dear. It is time for us to seek new sources of strength to sustain us that are consistent with our times, not times past.

I could argue that the god-concept does more harm than it does good. It explains nothing, but traps people into a way of thinking and an unhealthy fear. Neither is continuously worshiping God in a fixed reverential way a good use of the brain. It is a dumbing-down of the creative powers we have, looking backwards, not forwards. It is time to question old answers.

When I think of god at all –which is infrequent – it is a small-g god, the repository of all mystery, which is wondrous and complex beyond knowing, but not divine or an object of worship. To pretend otherwise is shear arrogance. I do not have any relation to a god concept and do not feel that any god-influences act in my life. In short, it is a carry-over from a primitive way of formulating answers and is an obstacle to newer formulations. But I am intrigued by the godless religions of the Far East that are built on respect for cultural values and not on fear and reward. Since the true meaning of religion is to build community, they seem to be closer to the idea of social interdependence than is the Western emphasis on individualism.

One thing is for sure. The organized church has become a powerful industry that sustains these mysticisms, miracles and superstitions as a basis of their own survival, diverting both energy and resources from the real issues of the day. It is very unlikely that they will give up this power base and source of income.

Thinking About Jesus

The earliest memories I have of Jesus were the wonderful impressions I received in a Baptist Sunday School. To my mind, he was all good. He helped, he shared, he comforted, and he taught, all in a soft way. I still have those good memories and will keep them for the rest of my life. For me, that is what religion is all about.

At the time, I had no idea of the conditions under which Jesus lived. For over four centuries, Israel had been dominated by the Babylonians, Egyptians, Greeks and Romans, respectively. Israel had come to the breaking point. Why did God let so much evil come to His chosen people?

Finally, in 170 B.C.E., the Book of Enoch called for a Messiah and the Kingdom of God. And shortly after, in 165 B.C.E., the Book of Daniel, cried out for a revolt. It foretells the fall of empires through the agency of God, not man, but "one like a son of man" will come on the clouds of heaven, embodying the apocalyptic hope of the Jews and accompanied by a general resurrection of the dead.

The Jews did revolt in 50 B.C.E. and again in 43 B.C.E. and lost both times to the Romans, who took 30,000 Jews into slavery. From 47 B.C.E. to 78 C.E., the times gave rise to five messiahs, 11 bandits, 10 prophets and 7 protestors and, of course, Jesus, all rebelling against Roman control. Jews firmly believed that God would not allow this evil to exist much longer and would bring in a kingdom of peace and justice.

It was this turmoil and apocalyptic expectation into which Jesus was born. It was the message that John the Baptist was preaching when he baptized Jesus. And it was the message that Jesus began preaching when John the Baptist was beheaded. Jesus believed in the apocalypse, the prevailing Jewish feeling that the world had become so terrible for the Jews that something had to give.

In this context, Jesus is best understood as an apocalyptic prophet who anticipated that God would soon intervene in the course of history to overthrow the forces of evil and bring in his good Kingdom on Earth. In 1906, Albert Schweitzer studied the teachings of Jesus and concluded that many of his sayings made no sense at all without understanding the apocalyptic urgency of the times. Jesus advised people to give up their jobs and follow him, to leave their families if they did not agree, and to give the coats off of their backs; all impractical things that made no sense unless the world was coming to an end.

I had questioned many of the extreme requests that Jesus made of his followers. I knew they did not seem practical in my life, even if I wanted to follow them, and I didn't know any devoted Christians who gave up their jobs or left their families. It was not until Schweitzer referred to them as "interim ethics" appropriate only to the apocalyptic expectation that things made sense.

It was a real Kingdom to be brought by God's special messenger, whom Jesus referred to as the Son of Man (quoting the Book of Daniel). The coming judgment would involve a destruction of the present order of things and a complete reversal of fortunes for the powerful and the oppressed. People needed to prepare for its coming, by repenting of their wrongdoings, giving up their power and wealth, and by living completely for others.

This last phrase is the only thing that ties in with my Sunday school lessons.

Needless to say, Jesus was a Jew and strongly believed in Judaism. He left no clue that he intended to form a new religion. He wrote nothing and encouraged his disciples to preach to the Jews and not the Gentiles. In the end, it could be argued that he provoked his own death, truly believing that he was signaling the beginning of the end of the world of evil and ushering in the Kingdom of peace and justice on earth for Israel.

There are absolutely no available writings between Jesus' death in about 30 C.E. and 49C.E. These two decades are commonly called the Unbridgeable Gap or the Lost Decades. As we will see later, the four gospels that are in the New Testament were not written until sometimes between 65 C.E. at the earliest and 130 C.E. at the latest. This gives us no insight into what was happening during and immediately after Jesus' death. There was no written material, no doctrine and no creed at that time. The missionaries went forth with an oral story as they remembered it.

Since we have only the Book of Acts as a very limited account of the early missionary years, the best we can do is to put ourselves in their sandals and try to understand what they encountered.

Let's say it's five years after Jesus' death and we get on the road with our oral traditions. What would we expect to encounter? We know that wherever we traveled, people would already have a culture, language, tradition, history and religion, maybe many. We doubt that they were anxious to see us coming and probably resented our imposing on them.

In Greece, we find the 13-century old religion of Cybele and Attis. It is believed that Attis was born of a virgin on December 25th, murdered, buried and rose from the dead after three days. Does this sound vaguely familiar to anyone?

In Rome, the mighty Roman army worshipped Mithras, the sun god, whose birthday was also on December the 25th. If this seems coincidental, it is because December the 25th is the time of the winter solstice and the lengthening of the days of sun. The army officers held their religious services on Sunday at which time they shared a sacred meal. Throughout the Roman Empire, Constantine made Sunday a day of rest, closing the law courts and forbidding any work except for agricultural labor in season.

Both the Greeks and the Romans celebrated Hilaria, a day of joy from which we get the word hilarious. It primarily celebrated the vernal equinox on March 25th to honor – who else -- Cybele. But the name was given to any day or season for rejoicing, private or public, including marriages, births, etc. After Constantine converted to Christianity in 312 C.E., he still commissioned a statue to the mother-Goddess Cybele, though she was presented in the posture of saying a Christian prayer.

Had we travelled to Egypt, we would have found that the followers of Isis adored a Madonna figure nursing her holy child.

And everywhere, we encountered virgin births. In Greece, it was Plato, Mithras, Attis and Alexander the Great. In Egypt, it was Horus and Ra. In India it was the Buddha, conceived when a divine power called the Holy Ghost descended on the virgin Maya. The Hindus claimed Christha, the Savior. The Sufis claimed the poet Kabir. In China, it was Lao-Tzu. In Taiwan, it was Colon. Virgin births were apparently bestowed as an honorarium for someone exceptional. I think this was a title also given to Jesus.

How should we proceed? Should we try to overthrow the existing religions and replace them? Not really. It is much easier to assimilate than to replace. In this case, we will retain the things that are not important to us and slowly introduce the things that are.

If fact, there are many appealing things about these religious practices that are worth adopting. We really don't know Jesus' birthday. Is there any harm in sticking with December the 25th? The Jews worshipped on the Sabbath, but is there anything wrong with worshiping on Sunday? The Roman army's sacred meal fits right in with our Last Supper and Communion. Couldn't we accept an image of the Virgin Mary caressing the young baby Jesus? And shouldn't we adopt a day of joy to celebrate the Resurrection around March 25th and call it Easter? We will gently rename their concepts to fit our purposes.

So many of the Christian practices are an amalgam of many cultural religions. The problem is that assimilation in different areas with different religions leaves you with different forms of Christianity. Not just a few, but many. For example, there were the Adoptionists, Archonticis, Arians, Barbelognostics, Carpocrates, Cerinthians, Congregation of Jesus, Donatists, Ebionites, Encratites, Gnostics, Hippolytus Community, John Community, Luke Community, Marcionites, Mark Community, Matthew Community, Meletians Community, Menandrians, Montanus Community, Nazarenes,

Ophites, Orthodox Community, Patripassianists, Pauline Community, Phibionites, Pillars of Jerusalem, Q Community, Quartodecimians, Stratiotics, the Thomas Community and many, many more.

We know that Bishop Filastrius compiled a list of 156 distinct so-called Christian sects. And no one knows if he knew them all. By 180 C.E. Bishop Ireneaus of Lyons had written a five-volume book entitled "Against Heresies." The Greek word "heresy" originally meant options, choices or alternatives. It did not acquire a pejorative connotation until the proto-orthodox used it against the alternative sects.

There were those who claimed that Jesus was born and died a human. Others thought he was born human, became divine when the dove descended during his baptism, remained divine during his ministry, and lost his divinity on the cross when he cried, "My God, my God, Why have you forsaken me?" Some claimed he was always God and left no footprints when he walked. Others claimed he couldn't be God, because a God cannot die and Jesus died on the cross. Some claimed he was born of a virgin. Others said he was born naturally as a twin with Jude.

The historian Paul Johnson put it this way: "Christianity began in confusion, controversy and schism and so it continued. The followers of Jesus were divided right from the start on elements of faith and practice. And the further the missionaries moved from the base, the more likely it was that their teachings would diverge. From the start there were numerous varieties of Christianity which had little in common, though they centered round belief in the resurrection."

So ends our imaginary mission. I think it is reasonable to assume that this is something like what the missionaries experienced and how they proceeded. But what are we to conclude from this? They were there and we are centuries away.

There is indirect evidence that various people were trying to remember and record the sayings of Jesus. The best known of these are the Book of Signs and the Lost Sayings Q Gospel (Q is short for quelle, the German word meaning source). They are indirectly known because the Synaptic Gospels of Mark, Matthew and Luke contain exact quotations that they could only get by having the same missing source books. Scholars deduced the existence of the Lost Sayings Q gospel but no copy has ever been found.

Another "sayings" book that was less used was the Gospel of Thomas. It was lost for centuries before it was found in Egypt in 1954. The Gospel of Thomas was a Gnostic Christian book. The Gnostics were one of 156 different Christian sects that competed to become the orthodox version of Christianity. I was thrilled when copies of this gospel were available and I could get a fresh insight into Jesus' ministry.

The Gospel of Thomas has 150 verses and 114 of them start with the words "Jesus said." This is a treasure and a new look at the early Jesus. The first verse of the Gospel of Thomas is as follows: "These are the obscure sayings that the living Jesus uttered and which Didymus Jude Thomas wrote down. "Whoever finds the meanings of these sayings will not taste death."

I was surprised to find that Didymus and Thomas are not names, as we think of Thomas today, but family relationship roles like sister, aunt or twin. Didymus is the Greek word for twin and Thomas is the Aramaic word for twin. This double emphasis that Jude was the twin brother of Jesus was totally new to me. I had never heard that Jesus had a twin and it brings up the issue about a virgin birth for one, both or neither. This strongly suggests that the author of this gospel was Jude, the twin brother of Jesus that is named in Mark 6:3 and John 21:2. This implies that it was written soon after Jesus' death while Jude was alive.

The Gospel presents the religion of Jesus and not a religion about Jesus, as Christianity would later convert it. It encourages the hearer not so much to believe in Jesus as to seek to know God through one's own divinely given capacity, since all are created in the image of God. In the Gospel, Jesus said, "the Kingdom of God is within you" and the way to salvation is to know your self and renounce the material world. Get there by living a holy life. Verse 3 of the Gospel of Thomas reads: "When you become acquainted with yourselves, then you will be recognized. And you will understand that it is you who are children of the living father. But if you do not become acquainted with yourselves, then you are in poverty, and it is you who are the poverty."

Reading Thomas made an enormous impression on me. It helped clarify what is meant by the kingdom of God. There are several conflicting meanings in the literature. The oldest relates to freeing the "Chosen People of God" from centuries of occupation and persecution. It was not the end of time but the end of evil that had beset the Jews and would usher in the Kingdom of God on earth for Israel. As Christianity spread, a broader interpretation held that the Kingdom is not limited to Israel, but is available to all Christian lands. But this was too broad; the Kingdom then became limited to those who accepted Christ as their savior. When the apocalypse never happened and the world did not come to an end, the Kingdom of God was conveniently moved to Heaven. Only Jesus said "The Kingdom of God is Within You." This definition was opposed by Paul, John and the subsequent church because it was a Gnostic concept implying that salvation comes only from self-knowledge. But I see this as the most profound definition; salvation not as external reward but internal reward from coming to know your self. And it is this understanding I identify with.

The phrase "the Kingdom of God is within you" is hauntingly consistent with the advice of the ancient Greeks to "Know Yourself" and the modern understanding that all the battles of life are waged within the self. Knowing the Gospel of Thomas was written by Jesus' twin shortly after his death, I want to accept this as Jesus' understanding of the Kingdom. It is meaningful to me now in this life.

Obviously these ideas did not fit the evolving theology of the church that was basically finalized in 381 C.E. at the Second Council of Constantinople under Emperor Theodosius, the Great.

It was only after the theology had been agreed to could the church fathers select books for the New Testament that supported the theology. Of the 118 books that are known today to have been available, only 27 were chosen. The four narratives of Jesus that were included constitute a mixed blessing for me and for scholars trying to understand the real Jesus because of their inconsistances.

The Gospel according to Mark was written by an anonymous author sometimes between 65 and 80 C.E., and is the first of the narrative gospels. It was written in upper class Greek while all the apostles spoke Aramaic. The original text contained 661 verses, 47 of which were identical to verses in the Gospel of Thomas. As an enormous corruption of the Gospel according to Mark, seventeen additional verses were added sometimes in the 11th Century to the last chapter to make it conform to the prevailing doctrine. We know this because none of the earlier manuscripts contained these verses.

The Gospel according to Matthew was written by an anonymous author sometimes between 80 and 100 CE in Greek. It contains 1010 verses, 600 identical to Mark, 17 from Thomas, and an unknown number from the Lost Sayings Q Gospel. Matthew was written to appeal to the Jews after the Temple was destroyed in 70 C.E. To entice the Jews to become Christians, the author took 40 prophesies from the Old Testament that the Messiah would have to fulfill and wrote them into the text as though Jesus had fulfilled them. This is the origin of many of the miracle stories.

The Gospel according to Luke was written by an anonymous author sometime between 80 and 130 CE in Greek. It contains 1146 verses, 350 taken from Mark, four from Thomas and an unknown number from the Lost Saying Q Gospel. The gospel was dedicated to a Roman official, Theophilus, to try to convince the Romans that Christianity was a peace-loving religion. It is by far the most gentle of the gospels, avoiding the internal disagreements and the fractious differences between the 156 competing splinter groups that wanted to be recognized as the true Christianity.

The Gospel according to John was written by an anonymous author sometime between 90 C.E. and 120 C.E., also in Greek. It contains 879 verses with nothing from Mark, Matthew or Luke and five verses from Thomas. It was apparently written to counter the growing influence of the Gnostics. It argues that you gain salvation by belief in Jesus, as Paul was preaching, not by gaining self-knowledge.

The practice of writing something and attributing it to another person is called pseudepigrapha. It was a common practice in the time of Jesus. There are several reasons for it. Some authors wanted to give credit to the individual who had the original ideas and not be accused of plagiarism. Some wanted to gain prestige and readership based on another person's prestige. And some did it simply to honor another. So all of the gospels carry the wording "according to" in their titles.

Getting back to Jesus' ministry, there is little doubt that he encouraged all to repent, follow him, and be ready for the end of the existing order – not the end of time – but the arrival of the Kingdom of God on earth: a spiritual Jewish nation without external conquerors.

From Paul's view, these activities implied struggle, violence, and Jewish nationalism. They were appropriate for Jesus' purposes, but they would not appeal to Roman, Greek or Egyptian audiences. Thus Paul had to envision a broader base for "his" universal religion.

Paul selected four tenets: (1) the urgency about the world coming to an end to get people's attention and encourage them to prepare for it, (2) the miracles of Jesus to woo them, (3) salvation through faith in Christ, and (4) a big-stretch interpretation of the Kingdom of God, namely the promise of an afterlife in Heaven.

Paul needed Jesus to be more than a teacher or prophet to the Jews. He needed a crowning presence to worship. So he elevated Jesus from a prophet to a messiah, a word that translates to Christ in Greek. But the words messiah or Christ do not mean god. It was not until 325 C.E. that the bishops at Nicaea finally elevated Jesus to being divine.

But the greatest re-interpretation of all for me was that Jesus was crucified to save us from our sins. This means he was sacrificed for us. However, the Roman Senate had outlawed human sacrifices as early as 97 B.C.E. The Roman officials knew this very well and crucified Jesus as a political agitator, not as a sacrificial lamb for all future sinners. Only the church would re-interpret this to suit their theology.

In one great turn of the wheel of history, Paul changed the religion from the teachings of Jesus to the worship of Christ. Paul hardly ever quoted Jesus in his preaching or writings. It was faith alone – belief in Jesus Christ – that provides salvation, not good works like Jesus did. I do not think for a minute that Paul was insensitive to the value of good works. Paul was a Jew who grew up honoring the moral laws of the prophets. I think he felt the enormous urgency of the eminent apocalypse and there was little time to perform good works. Hence, I am prone to think that he invoked" salvation by faith in Jesus" as a concession made to recruit converts fast and easily in a time of urgency. In any event, he created Christianity. He converted the religion of Jesus to a religion about Christ.

It was a great embarrassment to the early church fathers that the apocalypse didn't happen. They kept pushing the date out and making excuses why it had not come. Finally, the idea slowly faded quietly into history, except for a few ultra believers who anticipate it every thousand years and have always been wrong and maybe disappointed. But the big question is: How could Jesus have gotten that wrong if he was divine? It was the centerpiece of his ministry.

The Quest for the Historical Jesus

The 19th Century was known for its quest for the historical Jesus. It was driven by a thoroughly romantic Protestant obsession that the Catholic religion was a pagan adulteration of true Christianity. Protestant biblical scholars wanted to leap frog over two centuries and land at the "true" beginnings in the life and teachings of Jesus. But the only record at that time was the four gospels. The quest for the historical Jesus would swirl around (1) the miracles and (2) the disagreement between the four gospels. Some of the differing opinions are found in the following selected books.

- John Locke wrote *The Reasonableness of Christianity* in 1695.
- Hermann Reimarus wrote *The Intention of Jesus and His Disciples* about 1760.
- Constantin Volney wrote *Ruins of Empire* in 1791 questioning Jesus' existence.
- Thomas Jefferson wrote *The Jefferson Bible* in 1820, using a pen knife to remove all the miracles and keep the sayings.

- F. C. Barr wrote *The Christ Party in the Corinthian Community* about 1860 showing conflicts between Peter and Paul and between the Jewish and Gentile Christians.
- David Strauss wrote *The Life of Jesus Critically Examined* in 1835, separating the mystical from the historical.
- Johannes Weiss wrote *Jesus' Proclamation of the Kingdom of God* in 1892, showing Jesus as a radical visionary of a cataclysmic end.
- Albert Schweitzer wrote *The Quest of the Historical Jesus* in 1906, showing Jesus as an apocalyptic teacher whose ethic was an "interim ethic" before the cataclysmic end.
- Walter Bauer wrote *Orthodoxy and Heresy in Earliest Christianity* in 1934, showing struggles over power, not just theology.
- S. G. F. Brandon shows Jesus as a political revolutionary in 1967.
- Morton Smith shows Jesus as a magician in1978.
- Geza Vermes shows Jesus as a Galilean charismatic in 1984.
- Bruce Chilton shows Jesus as a Galilean rabbi in 1984.
- Harvey Falk shows Jesus as an Essene in 1985.
- Harvey Falk shows Jesus as a Hellenite Pharisee in 1985.
- E. P. Sanders shows Jesus as an eschatological prophet in 1985.
- John Hicks wrote "The Myth of God Incarnate" in 1991.
- John Dominic Crossan wrote *The Historical Jesus* in 1991. "Crossan's Jesus isn't gentle, meek, or mild. He is an illiterate peasant, both healer and social revolutionary without the Lord's Prayer, the Virgin Birth, or the Sermon on the Mount."
- Reza Aslan wrote *Zealot: The Life and Times of Jesus of Nazareth* in 2013.

The Jesus Seminar

In 1985, Robert W. Funk convened the Jesus Seminar to evaluate the historical significance of every shred of evidence about Jesus from antiquity (30 to 200 CE). The seminar held semi-annual meetings that were open to the public and recorded in detail.

Over 200 scholars worldwide have participated. Seminar Fellows are scholars with advanced degrees who must be able to read and interpret primary source material. About half the scholars come from Harvard, Claremont and Vanderbilt Universities.

They have examined over 1,500 sayings attributed to Jesus. Analysis ended with a secret ballot using four colored beads. A red bead was dropped into the voting box if the examined saying was believed to be authentic. A pink bead signified maybe yes; a gray bead signified maybe no; and a black bead signified definitely no. The conclusion was that less than 17% of the sayings are considered by scholars to be authentic. The Jesus Seminar published a version of the Bible in which the sayings attributed to Jesus are printed in the four colors indicating their opinion of authenticity: red, pink, gray and black.

It is hard to know what to make of this confusing and contradictory summary. I can sense the scholars and writers are easing away from the traditional view of Jesus as a placid miracle worker. One thing it has done for sure: it has shattered the meek and mild image of Jesus I learned in Sunday school. The picture of Jesus has been made infinitely more complex by seeing his role in the traumatic politics of his time and the anticipated apocalypse that never occurred.

I believe the church has corrupted the true understanding of the historical Jesus, probably beyond reconstruction, for its own purposes. For me, it comes down to this. I do not believe that Jesus is or was divine or part of a god-head. My respect for natural law does not allow me to accept the virgin birth, the miracles, the resurrection, the ascension, the concepts of heaven and hell or the need for salvation.

I see Jesus as a Jew who had great concerns for his religion and the future of Israel. And I can understand how others have capitalized on his ministry as the basis of forming a new religion in his name. But going from a religion of Jesus to a religion about Jesus, is too big of a jump for me. Too much detail gets lost in the translation for me and apparently for many practicing Christians. On what basis do I speak for Christians? Well, the number of Christian sects went from 156 to one in 325 C.E. Since then it has blossomed to 41,000 different Christian sects today, according to Google. Apparently many practicing Christians have a different slant on what Christianity actually is.

Theology by Political Process

In retirement, I read Dan Brown's novel *The Da Vinci Code* and came away, like so many others, not knowing what parts were history and what parts were fiction. It left me excited and a little embarrassed. I had been brought up in a Judeo-Christian heritage and had not been exposed to these ideas in my many years of Sunday school and church life.

So I decided to do something about it by reading early church history. I soon found how little I knew about the true origins of Christianity. As I mentioned previously, there is no written history from the death of Jesus till 49 C.E. Scholars like John Dominic Crossan and others have spent much of their working lives trying to finesse out from indirect evidence about what was really happening.

The earliest reference we have is Paul going to Jerusalem in 49 C.E. to argue with Peter and James about converting the gentiles. Shortly afterwards, Paul wrote his first letter to the Thessalonians in 51 C.E. There is no question that Paul was motivated and highly active in spreading his version of proto-Christianity, namely the world is coming to an end during his lifetime and there is no time to gain salvation except by having faith in Christ.

This is the theology that is so familiar to us because it finally won out. But out of the 156 sects there were also competing theologies.

Marcion argued that God and Christ were two different entities. He observed that God of the Old Testament was of a wrathful, judgmental, vindictive nature. By contrast Jesus was a divine being with a loving, compassionate nature. He preached that these two must be different gods and this view was very popular.

The Adoptionist argued that Jesus was human in every way,

including being born of sexual union of Mary and Joseph. Jesus was simply more righteous than all others so God appointed him – adopted him – to be his son and do his work.

The Patripassianist believed that God actually came to earth and became Jesus.

Arian of Alexandria argued that God the Father created Christ as God the Son in eternity past and then Christ created all things. Christ then became human by being born of a virgin, died for our sins, raised from the dead and returned to heaven. This view was extremely popular.

This condition of theological differences grew and festered for almost three centuries with each sect defiantly professing that they had the correct interpretation. It was not until 312 C.E. when Constantine won the battle of Milvian Bridge that he converted to Christianity. In 324 C.E., he defeated his co-emperor, Licinius, and became the sole Emperor of the Roman Empire.

Having been asked repeatedly to resolve issues between the various Christian sects, Constantine called the first church council in 325 C.E., roughly 300 years after Jesus' death. It was held in Nicaea, close to his imperial capital in Constantinople. He invited all 1800 bishops, but only 318 bishops and their delegations attended. It started on May 19th and would last for a very long month. In essence he told the bishops that there was only one Roman Empire and only one Emperor and there should be only one Christianity. He invited them to debate until they agreed on which one. And he promised that whatever theology the church decided on, the state would enforce it.

Constantine played an active role. It was he who declared December 25th the birthday of Jesus, most probably to satisfy his army.

The debates were long and hostile. They lasted so long that the great majority in the middle lost interest and wanted this to be resolved so they could go home. It finally boiled down to the nature of Jesus -- human or divine -- with Arian claiming Jesus was human and the Athanasius claiming he was divine.

The Arians argued the rational view that Christ was human and subordinate to God so we could retain monotheism. It was argued that if Jesus were human, his miracles and teachings were magnificent. But if he were a god, his activities were rather lukewarm compared with what one would expect of a superhuman god.

On the other hand, Athanasius argued the paradoxical view that Jesus was both simultaneously human and divine. He wanted to maintain monotheism to appeal to the Jews and he wanted Jesus to be a god to replace the pagan gods to appeal to the Greeks. This was strictly a political strategy. After much debate, and with the majority in the middle losing interest and bowing out, Athanasius won. And as of June 325 C.E. the orthodox position was that there were two persons making one god, each equal in substance and co-equal, not two gods but one god manifest in two persons.

This conclusion did not satisfy the minority. Many left the church and became the famed Monks of the Desert. Others who argued for the Arian position left and formed new religions that exist to this day. One sect was so disappointed that they went into their church building, locked the doors, and voluntarily burnt the building down with the members inside. It was not a charitable compromise.

Constantine did not keep his promise. The Bishop Eusebius of Nicomedia convinced Constantine that the "two in one, but only one" was logically indefensible and that his name would be associated with the illogic forever. Constantine immediately reversed his allegiance, became an Arian Christian, exiled Athanasius and banished most of the Nicene leaders. Constantine was baptized on his deathbed in 337 C.E. by Bishop Eusebius of Nicomedia as an Arian Christian. Constantine believed that being baptized washed away all your sins – of which he had many -- so he smartly waited until he was dying to be baptized.

When Constantine's three sons took over the empire, the oldest son favored Nicene Christianity and recalled Athanasius and the others from exile.

But when the oldest son was killed in battle, the youngest son favored Arian Christianity and again exiled Athanasius.

The youngest son also consecrated Ulfinas as an Arian Bishop and sent him to become the "apostle" to the Goths. Ulfinas deserves special mention. The Goths had no written language. So Ulfinas created the Teutonic alphabet and wrote the first book in the Teutonic language. The Goths loved and respected him and became Arian Christians.

When the middle son returned from battle, the youngest son was forced to follow a more moderate policy and Athanasius was allowed to return.

Finally, the middle son was killed in battle and the youngest pro-Arian son became sole emperor in 350 C.E. Jerome said "the entire world woke from a deep slumber and discovered that it had become Arian." Once again the Nicene leaders had to leave their cities and even the Bishop of Rome (the Pope) signed an Arian confession of faith. Arianism was at its peak in 361 C.E. At a Council in Sirmium, the leaders completely rejected the decisions made in Nicaea in 325 C.E.

Later that year, 361 C.E., the last son of Constantine died and the next emperor, Julian the Apostate, rejected all Christianity and tried to return the Roman Empire to its glorious days of paganism. But Julian was killed in battle just two years later in 363 C.E.

Emperor Jovian followed Julian. Jovian was an admirer of Athanasius, and returned him from exile. But Jovian only lived a few months.

Emperor Valens followed Jovian and was a staunch defender of Arianism. And so the type of Christianity continued to be a political yo-yo for 56 years.

I find this very unsettling that the theology of the church was bouncing around in the hands of the state. And what became the final Christian theology was only a question of which emperor "voted" last. And the last to "vote" was Emperor Theodosius the Great who followed Valens. If they couldn't decide if Jesus was divine, I certainly can't.

Theodosius had bigger things to worry about than theological squabbles. The Roman Empire was surrounded by threatening barbarians: Goths, Vandals, Barbers, and Huns. He wanted to put the Christian issue to bed so he could concentrate on the defense of the Empire.

So in 381 C.E., Theodosius the Great, who favored the Nicene Christianity, summoned the Council of Constantinople and declared the Nicene Creed as the only orthodox one. At the same council the Holy Spirit was declared to be divine and was added to the Son and the Father forming the Holy Trinity. Emperor Theodosius made this revised form of Christianity the state religion of the Roman Empire and enforced it with all the terrors of the law. And that is how we got the Trinitarian Christianity we have today: by political process and state enforcement. This does not leave me comfortable at all.

In his Easter Letter of 367 C.E., Athanasius of Alexandria proposed 27 books to be included in the New Testament. After the orthodox theology was resolved in 381 C.E., this selection of books was confirmed at the Third Council of Carthage in 419 C.E. However, with all the controversies, doctrinal tweaks, and Biblical "editing" of the Middle Ages, the Catholic Church did not give final approval for the New Testament until provoked by the Protestant Reformation at the Council of Trent in 1545. And the first version to have chapters and verses was the Geneva Edition published in 1560.

After 419 C.E., Athanasius ordered all the rest of the early Christian books to be destroyed. And most were. This is not the first time in history or the last that a person in power destroyed books that offended him. However, I find this an unforgivable act to deny history the prevailing thoughts of the time and to destroy books that were cherished by many.

Some Gnostic bishops so loved the rejected books that they ignored the order and buried some of them in the Egyptian soil where the environment was hot and dry and the books would be preserved. One collection of these books was discovered at Nag Hammani in 1954, including the Gospel of Thomas and a few other invaluable gospels. Over the years, a reasonable number of these rejected books have been found in monasteries, libraries and, yes, graves. I can only hope that other collections will be found in the future.

Mohammed thought the idea of the Trinity was so offensive that he founded Islam in 632 C.E. declaring that there was only one god, Allah, and Jesus was a prophet. When Islam spread west, the Arian

Christians from Egypt to Spain welcomed the Muslims and easily converted because they too believed in only one god with Jesus as a human.

In Europe, arguments continued. From 429 to 810 C.E. there were at least ten major councils involved with theological word-smithing. The last, the Filioque Controversy of 810 C.E., concerned itself with the question whether the Holy Spirit came from God and through Jesus or did the Holy Spirit come from both God and Jesus.

You can imagine that after all the effort to get the theology just right, the Church didn't want anyone to mess with it. But people did mess with it. And I would have too. The irrational idea of a Trinity caused many to start rethinking the theology. Sects rose in France and Spain called the Albigensians, Waldensians and Cathars, but the church called them heretics. The Church tried for ten years to teach them to return to the main stream. But they would not return. So the Church organized a crusade against wayward Christians from 1205 to 1229 C.E.. It was known as the Albigenses Crusade. For seven years, Southern France was devastated by one of the most bloodthirsty wars in history. The Albigenses were slaughtered by the thousands and their property was confiscated. Then the Crusaders moved to Spain and massacred the Cathars at Beziers.

Two years later, in 1231 C.E., the infamous Inquisition was established which lasted until the late 1800s. Its job was to investigate the inhabitants, examine their religious beliefs and decide if their beliefs were heretical.

Starting in 1252 C.E., the inquisitors were permitted to torture subjects and the practice of burning convicted heretics alive was put into canonical law.

What I conclude from this very brief historical review is that much of the theology and practices of the modern church were established by debate, and enforced by the state and the Inquisition. For over a half century Christian theology was treated like a yo-yo depending on which emperor was in power. I don't find any confidence in establishing sacred theology by a political process. It does not inspire me to believe in the eternal and cosmic truth of a theology so derived.

I am appalled at the violence and cruelty that was perpetrated by the church on people who chose to think differently. Knowing how capriciously the theology was crafted, it is hard to defend the righteousness of their position at the cost of human life.

Lastly, in the modern church, no one prays to Emperor Theodosius, the Great, but it is he who determined the final theology of Christianity. Personally, I think he made a grand mistake. Accepting the rational Arian position would have avoided the many indefensible debates and the needless bloodshed.

I do not believe in the Christian theology because it is so counter to all the rational evidence to the contrary.

The date when the last nation in Europe ended the Inquisition was 1890. I was born in 1930, just 40 years later. I have no doubt that if I were having the thoughts I have a century earlier, and especially, putting them into print, I would be in serious trouble or maybe worse.

Morality, Spirituality and Religion

It is interesting that the words morality, spirituality and religion are used almost interchangeably by most organized religions. It is as though they are three aspects of the same thing. Certainly the church wants to be seen as the essence of spirituality although there are many, many churches and I can only conceive of one form of spirituality. And churches envision themselves as the champions and guardians of morality, except when it serves their interest to be immoral.

I see these three words as being different and orthogonal. By orthogonal, I mean they are 100% independent of each other. This is a clear distinction from the way that the church has traditionally merged them together for its benefit. But I see them as unique and separate. Let me expand on this.

In his book entitled *The Faith Instinct*, Nicholas Wade develops the case that morality is older than religion. Its roots can be seen in monkeys and apes that have no religions. Biologists have come to realize that social animals, in interacting with other members of their community, have developed rules for restraining their self-interest. These are the rules of self-restraint that are likely to have a genetic basis. Only in the human species have we grafted religion on top of our internal moral compass.

Morality, for me, has a sense of inner direction to do no harm. I have come to believe that the moral code is an epiphenomenon of the genetic code. It is built in our genetic makeup to understand that joint survival is becoming as important as individual survival. Living in a complex society, many of the threats to life are common to all of us. We have evolved mirror neurons that have us react to the misfortunes of others. We sense another person's pain and feel empathy and sympathy. We see small children help their siblings and playmates long before they attend church or are trained in morals. For me, basic morality emanates from the human, not from the outside.

Churches may encourage people to live up to their inner morality, but so do the Boy Scouts and the Masons. But morality is not the same as religion. People who do not have any exposure to religion or churches still have an inner sense of morality. Hence morality is independent of religion.

Likewise, spirituality is an innate quality of the human. I do not like the word spirituality because in our culture it can easily be mistaken for a relationship with the supernatural concept of spirits, as in ghosts, goblins, angels and devils. By spirituality, I mean the ability to be inspired: to have an inner spirit with ready enthusiasm. It is true that I can be inspired by the church with its rituals, its reverence and messages. But I can also be inspired by many other things, such as nature, national loyalty, lasting friendships and even my favorite sports teams.

Spirituality, for me, does not relate to external spirits, but to the internal spirit of the individual. It is élan and the capacity to appreciate, an invitation to wonder and a lesson in humility. For many people the wonders of nature bring out a sense of awe that could be described as spiritual with no connection to morality or religion.

Admiring nature could be interpreted as a religious feeling if nature were created by a supernatural force. But it wasn't. Nature is the working out of natural laws. I, too, stand in awe of the beauty and majesty of nature. I find nature inspiring and at times breathtaking. And I wonder about the mystery of its origins and development. But I think of these in terms of natural laws, not in supernatural terms. I appreciate the emotional boost I receive from the drama of nature, but I don't think to worship it in a religious way. Spirituality is personal. It is the inner capacity to be inspired.

Some people relegate the notion of spirituality to the ultra-extreme examples, such as the proverbial guru, isolated on a mountain-top, contemplating the essence of life or Emily Dickenson sitting isolated in her bedroom trying to express in poetry the ephemeral aspects of existence. While they are extreme examples, they are both expressions of an inner quality of wonder and satisfy my definition of spirituality. In both cases, neither is building community (religion) nor standing in right relationship with others (morality).

Religion stems from the Greek work "religio" which means to bind together, to build community. Churches, regardless of denomination, certainly do this. They bond people together for a specific purpose and they do it well.

But so does the political ward boss in Chicago. He bonds people together and builds community. He not only gets his constituents out to vote, he helps people get jobs, and serves the needs of the neglected. But you would not think of this as being spiritual or moral.

Religion does not own morality or spirituality. It embraces them. It uses them to advance its cause. But morality and spirituality are independent of religion and independent of each other.

My mother was the most moral person I know. She was a caring person who never offended others or spoke unkindly. She was hurt badly by two institutional churches and settled into a personal faith. She was also a practical, down-to-earth person and had little time for the gossamer side of life although she thrilled to artistic needlework. In her example of morality without religion or much spirituality, I rest my case.

For me the doctrine of the church holds captive both morality and spirituality. Many organized religions would have you believe that the three are synonymous. But they are separate, independent things. In my studied opinion you can be moral and/or spiritual without being religious.

The Basic Bargain

The basic bargain of religion is that in exchange for your believing in the doctrine and supporting the church now, it will enhance your social status in life and provide you an eternal life after death. It's a good deal, if true.

It makes no difference what the religion is, so long as you identify with it. Whether you are born into India's Buddhism, China's Confucianism, Iran's Islam, Belgium's Catholicism or the many Protestant denominations, you generally devote yourself with tenacity to the religion into which you are born. But each of us cannot have the luck of the draw to be born into the "right" religion. It is only the investment of myself that makes my church the "right" one.

Truth be told, theology has little to do with the "correctness" of a religion and everything to do with the fact that I place my hope in it. Said another way, it is the correct religion because I invest myself in it. I can change churches and it will again be the new correct religion because I again invest myself in it. I have done this three times in my life, and I know for sure. My investment causes the believability of the church. When you change churches you carry forward your personal investment. It is with our choice of churches that we are betting on receiving social acceptability and an afterlife in heaven, not the church's ability to deliver.

No religion can guarantee respect. Social acceptance is not so easily obtained as by attending church. Respectability comes from standing in right relationship to others and is independent of religion. It comes from having character, being open, being available, and achieving a responsible balance between your needs and those of others.

Neither can any religion promise life after death. It can promise hope. It can romance you with beauty and high-mindedness to support the idea. It can repeat with vigor the myths of the ancient past. But it cannot make good on its part of the bargain. At least, there is absolutely no evidence for it to date. And scientific advances are constantly undermining the possibility of eternal life.

It comes down to this. The fear of rejection and the fear of the unknown are the greatest fears that people have. The ambiguity that results drives people to find possible answers. But I am not sure that the church can do more than put band-aids on these fears. It certainly cannot guarantee answers.

I do not believe the basic bargain can be fulfilled. Clearly, respect is earned through serving. And my doubt of having an after-life energizes me to make the most of the one and only life I have. I think people dedicate too many hours and too many resources to support their existential hopes, hours and dollars that could be spent relieving real suffering.

Part II

Reflecting on the Present

Bottom-up Approach to Truth

My little adventure into early church history resulted in a big surprise. The Institute for Continued Learning (ICL) at Roosevelt University asked me to prepare and teach a course on what I had learned. Apparently there were others who had read *The DaVinci Code* and were interested. ICL is a non-degreed program for seniors who want to stay mentally and socially active. To every ones' amazement, 77 people signed up for the course, the largest attendance for any class at either campus in the history of the University.

I repeated the nine-week class for three semesters, always with large attendances. However, this became a bit repetitious for me, and, frankly, it didn't address the DaVinci Code quandary. So I suggested having more courses moving forward in history. The suggestion was well received and I had a faithful following that stayed with me for eight years as we progressively examined the history of Western Civilization. The following courses progressively included The Age of Faith, The Renaissance, The Protestant Reformation, The Age of Reason, The Enlightenment, The Influence of the Enlightenment in Colonial America, The Age of Ideology, The Age of Revolution, The Age of Cultural Wars, The Age of Science (Parts 1 and 2) and the Age of Neuroscience (Parts 1, 2, 3, & 4).

One of the most fascinating observations I distilled from this exploration was the evolving approach to the pursuit of truth.

Revelation is most probably the earliest approach to truth. Ancient men felt that God Himself had spoken to them and delivered eternal cosmic truth. This is the ultimate "top-down" example of defining truth. Of course, there were various gods in various cultures revealing different truths. So we are on somewhat shaky grounds.

Societal rule probably came next. There were kings and rulers who tried to stabilize society by pronouncing laws that implied an underlying truth. I think of Nebuchadnezzar and the great stone with his code of laws. It was another form of "top-down" reasoning, an example of humans trying to understand and regulate the global complexities of life.

Then we had philosophical approaches. My favorite is Plato and his book entitled *Timaeus*. It is based on dualism, a simplistic way of seeing everything as two opposites. As mentioned earlier, the Persian prophet Zoroaster founded Zoroastrianism, a religion based on dualism, a theology of opposites: good and evil, day and night, hot and cold, up and down, life and death, etc. In the 4th Century B.C.E., Plato conceived of a cosmology based on dualism. He had a fictional astronomer named Timaeus present the following argument. Since there is one domain, Earth, in which all things are transient, there must be another domain where things are permanent. Since we are down here, it must be up there. Because things on Earth die, things up there must be eternal. On Earth we do not have perfect knowledge, so up there they must have perfect knowledge. We did not create the Earth, therefore it was created by someone up there. We have no gods on Earth, hence the gods must live up there.

If this sounds vaguely familiar, it was adopted as the cosmology of the Christian Church. Philosophy became theology. They changed only two things. Instead of many gods, they chose only one to conform with Judaic monotheism. And instead of the one God remaining in isolation, they had Him intervene with human affairs. Again it is a "top-down" approach trying to understand what is true.

Dualism is primitive and unsophisticated by modern standards. It is the grossest of generalizations. All life is lived in the gray area between the extremes. Dostoevsky wrote that the line between good and evil goes through the middle of each of us. All nuances and judgments, all cultural refinements and all difficult decisions lie between the extremes.

By 350 B.C.E., Aristotle, the best-known student of Plato, wrote a book – one of his 28 books – entitled *The Organum* on how to arrive at the truth. We know that *The Organum* was written in three parts, but only the first part, the Logic, seems to have been known to the Latin Christian world. Aristotle's basic argument was to rely on the ultimate authority and to use deductive logic to draw conclusions. And what was this ultimate authority? It was the supernatural authority of the gods and their teachings found in Timaeus' perfect domain. It was totally a "top-down" approach to truth.

One can see how a philosophy that emphasizes the ultimate, eternal things complements religion. Both Muslim and Christian clerics found Aristotle's Logic a convenient way to legitimize their theologies. Thomas Aquinas in the 12th Century was the most famous theologian to weave Aristotelian logic into Christian faith, producing a tapestry of philosophy and theology that is still accepted by the Catholic Church today. At the Council of Trent in 1545, the theology of Aquinas with its Aristotelian influence superseded that of St. Augustine. Some theologians even argue that God sent Aristotle to develop a logic in anticipation of Christianity's need.

The early Protestants had no problem equating ultimate authority with the Scriptures. But at the time of Aristotle, the New Testament had not been written and the Old Testament had not been assembled beyond the Torah. With the sophistication of the Greek philosophers and the clannish orientation of the "chosen people," it is unlikely that Aristotle was referring to the Hebrew writings. We still do not know what authority he had in mind.

Believing you have the truth with no proof can be incredibly dangerous. When the human mind opens the door to the supernatural – revelation, miracles and so forth – it also opens the door to the occult. Non-rational forces can be either good or bad. In 1646, Sir Thomas Browne required 652 pages to list and briefly treat the superstitions of the day.

Western history continued to flounder with its search for a better approach to the truth. They could not continue with the widespread beliefs in things unknown and unknowable. Something had to give. And give it did. Around 1600, a few individuals realized that very little progress had been made through the long years of the Middle

Ages using the top-down methods of the past. These were religious men who believed that if God created the world His fingerprints would be left in the creation. It was only necessary for them to examine each part of the creation by using a "bottoms-up" approach to find ultimate reality.

By 1620, a date I call the turning point in Western Civilization, Sir Francis Bacon wrote a book that he called *The New Organum*, thumbing his nose at Aristotle, the Aristotelian scholasticism and the church of his day. Aristotelian scholasticism is a "teaching" technique where harmony is sought between an accepted authoritative position and a conflicting position, said conflicting position being maneuvered to agree with the accepted authority.

Francis Bacon inverted the apple cart, turning the search for truth upside down. He said we should NOT start at the top with presumed authority but at the bottom with nature. Nature is God's handiwork and we should study it, measure it and come to understand it. From our findings we should draw preliminary conclusions using inductive methods. Then, because the mind is prone to error, we must test the generalizations experimentally. From the findings that prove to be repeatable, we should use inductive logic to seek higher generalizations, again to be tested and retested. Ultimately he thought this process would reveal the very "signature of God."

Will Durant wrote in *The Story of Civilization, Book VII*: "His *Novum Organum* proposed a new organ and system of thought – the inductive study of nature itself through experience and experiment. Though this book too was left incomplete, it is, with all its imperfections, the most brilliant production in English philosophy, the first clear call for an Age of Reason."

Quote from Bacon's book: "Human knowledge as we have it is a mere medley of ill-digested mass, made up of much credulity and much accident, and also of the childish notions which are at first imbibed. Therefore we must, at the start, clear our minds, so far as we can, of all preconceptions, prejudices, assumptions, and theories; we must turn away even from Plato and Aristotle, we must sweep out of our thoughts the "idols," or time-honored illusions and fallacies, born of our personal idiosyncrasies of judgment or the traditional beliefs and dogmas of our group; we must banish all logical tricks of wishful thinking, all verbal absurdities of obscure thought. We must put behind us all those majestic deductive systems of philosophy that proposed to draw a thousand eternal verities out of a few axioms and principles. There is no magic hat in science; everything taken from the hat must first be put into it by observation or experiment. And not by mere casual observation, not by simple enumeration of data, but by experience sought from experiment."

Bacon proposed a laborious induction by accumulation of all facts pertinent to a problem, their analysis, comparison, classification, and correlation, and, "by a due process of exclusion and rejection," the progressive elimination of one hypothesis after another, until the "form" or underlying law and essence of a phenomenon should be revealed. Knowledge of the "form" would give increasing control of the event, and science would gradually remake the environment and possible man himself.

I want us to be absolutely sure we know what a "bottom-up" approach to the truth consists of. In my opinion, this is the ultimate turning point in history.

There is a tale that Galileo dropped two balls from the Leaning Tower of Pisa. We now know that the tale is not true, but it illustrates the point. Before Galileo's time, people thought that a large ball would fall to the earth faster than a small ball. But in the tale, Galileo didn't try to reason about this. He conducted a simple experiment consisting of carrying the two balls to the top of the tower and dropping them. To everyone's surprise, they hit the ground at the same time. Argument over! The tale isn't true, but the physics of falling bodies is.

In short, he let the two balls tattle-tale on themselves. That is the way that "bottom-up" truth seeking works. You disengage your opinion and set up a situation in which a little part of nature "does its thing" under controlled conditions (meaning no other influences) and then you record what it did. Then someone else, independent of you, does the same thing to see if he confirms your findings. After many, many repeats, the finding gains believability and progressively moves from a hypothesis, to a theory and finally to a law of nature. Caution! This doesn't mean it is true and cast in concrete. If new information is found, the process starts all over again.

We will never know if the great natural scientists of that age ever read Bacon's words, but it appears that Bacon captured the spirit of the times. It also spurred the invention of new instruments to make such investigations possible. That era produced an incredible number of now famous names like Copernicus, Galileo, Harvey, Newton and a list that goes on in an unbroken chain to the present times. This is how the modern world came to understand acceleration, refraction, magnetism, blood circulation, electricity, radiation, etc. To dwell on these accomplishments would be traffic in the obvious. Our modern lifestyles depend almost totally on these "bottom-up" truths.

But developing the experimental method never dissuaded the philosophers from trying. The temptation to think their way to truth never slowed down. There were Hume and Kant, Hegel and Marx, Kierkegaard and Schopenhauer to name a few who continued to think their way to big-picture, top-down answers. And none of them agreed with each other. And they are relics of mainstream knowledge.

The take home message from this slice of history can be presented in a simple picture, shown below. It has two horizontal, parallel lines (floor and ceiling) each representing time moving from the left to the right.

The top line is labeled "Top down approaches to truth." From the top-down line, dangling like icicles, are all the major religions, philosophies, belief systems, political systems, economic systems, prejudices, superstitions, etc. that were pontificated from on high but not tested or confirmed. These are all products of the human mind trying to think through massive issues.

The bottom line is labeled "Bottom up approaches to truth." From the bottom line there are vertical lines like telephone poles representing the accomplishments achieved by the experimental methods. This approach to truth requires researchers with patience and skills to get one small part of nature to "confess" how it works.

They didn't assume or dictate; they "asked" in the only language nature knows. And from this effort, we have revealed the secrets of nature like magnetism, heredity, chemistry, DNA, etc. Each of these is a product of experimentation and confirmation.

Top-down Approaches to truth

Philosophies Religions, Politics

Bias-free experimental Methods

Bottom-Up Approaches to Truth   1620 C.E.

Now comes the fun. When I ask people if they accept the bottom-up truths they are unanimous in saying yes. So I go into detail. Do you believe in gravity that you cannot see? Yes; of course. Well, do you believe in electricity that you cannot see? Yes again. Well, do you believe in the germ theory of infection that is invisible to the eye? Emphatically yes. And so it goes on and on. They do not pick and choose .

So I go to different cultures and get the same responses. I go to different nations and get the same responses. I go to different religious advocates and get the same responses. This agreement is worldwide, regardless of culture, religion or politics.

Finally there is something that the whole world can agree on.

And do you know why? Because they are all established by a bottoms-up approach to truth. We are now making progress.

But when I ask people about the so-called "top-down truths," I rarely get agreements. Being specific, I ask "Do you believe in Keynesian economics?" "Do you believe in the Hindu faith?" "Do you believe in spirits or angels?" "Do you believe our justice system is fair?" Most often I get disagreements and often violence. Individuals may accept one "icicle" or another, typically their own religion or their political party, but I think we all know why that is. And they reject all the others. What is going on here? Why do some people invest so much emotion in a specific belief system that cannot be confirmed rationally or experimentally and is roundly rejected by others? I believe it is from habit, tradition and narcissism. It is potentially good for them, unlike bottom up truths that are good for everyone.

It is safe to say that differences between postulated systems proposed from top-down have been the major cause of wars and violence throughout history.

Truths established by experimentation are universally accepted, not just "believed" in. These proven concepts do not arouse emotions or lead to violence. They are consistent and you can plan on them with 100% confidence. How can we build a future world based on these methods?

I firmly believe in the bottom-up approach to truth. Most of the advantages of our modern life are based on these bias-free conclusions. It is hard to imagine a world without "bottom-up approaches to truth" and it is increasingly hard to suffer a world with "top-down approaches to truth."

There are issues that do not lend themselves yet to bottom-up analysis. Perhaps we will get another Francis Bacon with an advanced method to address these social issues. But until that time comes and from the small analysis we have made here, I have to tip my hat toward experimentation in the pursuit of truth and the rejection of all "icicles."

The Limits to Thinking

Metrology is the science of measurement. A thumb rule in metrology is to use a tool that is at least ten times more precise than what is being measured to gain accuracy. We do not think of our brain as a tool, and we certainly don't impose this rule when we use it. But our brains are the tools we use for measuring thoughts and drawing conclusions. It is laughable that we think the brain is capable of handling any subject. Let me share a few limitations we should understand.

Everyone knows that we can only speak one thing at a time. As complex as the brain is and as many parallel functions as it processes, it seems strange that we can only speak one thing at a time. It is the basis of a lot of Jewish grandmother jokes, like the one where she gives two sweaters to her grandson – one red and one green – and asks which he likes better. Regardless of which one he mentions, she can milk guilt from the situation by crying and asking what he doesn't like about the other.

Likewise, we can only think one thought at a time. People want to believe that they can think about multiple things at the same time. The popular term is multi-tasking. But the brain can't multi-task. We can jump from one thought to another in rapid-fire order, enough to make us think we are holding two thoughts at the same time. But we aren't. This is often called "monkey mind." In fact it slows us down. It takes the brain a finite amount of time to clear the memory registers and pull up a new memory.

Not only is language linear, the order in which the words are presented makes a big difference. Listeners start sensing the emotional content of words in the order they are presented. Many arguments are started before someone has completed a sentence. I am reminded of the husband who said that he and his wife had words, but he didn't get to use his.

Because of the serial nature, thoughts and language are linear and cannot convey what is happening in a dynamic world where everything changes in parallel. It is like taking still pictures in a movie theater with an infinite number of screens all showing at the same time. Thoughts and speech are simply limitations of the structure of the brain.

Because of the linearity, thoughts and language are static and cannot handle time-dependent concepts that are constantly changing. Suppose you are writing about a fast moving sports event or the lava flow from a volcano. You can write about it, but you can't express its active motion. The situation moves before you can complete the sentence. Have you ever noticed how fast sports announcers talk trying to keep up with the action? And they can only talk about one player or one event at a time. We are only safe coupling static words.

Our brains evolved through progressive chance mutations to adapt to the problems of yester-year. Our survival attests to their success. It is humorously said that we are capable of solving problems we will never have again, but incapable of solving tomorrow's problems except by chance. One of my favorite oxymorons is the expression "foreseeable future." Have you ever looked at some of the predictions that were made a hundred years ago?

There is also a limit to the creative powers of the mind. When movie producers try to create scary monsters, they seem to be limited to exaggerating the eyes, ears, nose, mouths, claws and other body parts of human-like figures. They are simply distorted images of people. Even the new wave of transformer movies create huge and threatening, machine-like structures of recognizable human-like figures.

During the Cold War, the Russian government complained that their science fiction writers could not dream up new concepts far enough ahead to keep their scientists inspired.

The brain can easily solve single variable problems, that is, one subject with two options, like should we eat at home or eat out. But when the number of variables increases, the brain cannot simultaneously solve a multiple-variable problem. This may sound insulting, but let's consider an example.

Suppose you plan to re-seed your lawn and want to get the best growth. I'm going to introduce four variables: seed type, fertilizer type, planting depth and watering time. You can choose between seed types A or B. You can choose between fertilizer C or D. You can plant the seeds to a depth or E or F. And you can water G or H minutes a week.

I'm sorry to tell you, but you have no way of knowing the interaction of these variables. You cannot possibly think your way to an answer. Over a hundred years ago, a British statistician named Fischer was trying to solve this very problem to help maximize his country's crop yield. He had to resort to experimentation. Two possibilities for each of four variables gives you 16 different combinations. So he prepared 16 different planting plots in an orthogonal pattern and planted each with different combinations of seeds, fertilizers, soil depth and watering time. Orthogonal means at right angles to each other so that unwanted effects cancel out mathematically.

Only when he cut the grass from each of the 16 plots and weighed the clippings could he tell which combination was best. The problem is that these variables interact with each other dynamically. By planting the plots in an orthogonal way, he could separate the variables mathematically like peeling an onion. He could tell you what percentage of the growth was attributable to the seed type, what percentage was attributable to the fertilizer type and so on. For illustration, the maximum grass growth could result from the combination of BCFH. Of course, if the lawn was sloped so some of the water would run off, you could get a different combination. Or if the seeds were not planted deep enough, the birds could feast on your seeds and you would get a different combination again. There is no way that the human brain can prejudge the outcome of such a situation.

Fischer built on this idea and introduced a significant new field of mathematics known as the Design of Experiments. I taught Design of Experiments at Motorola University. It is used in industry to get machines to "talk" to them. We do it by setting controls on machines at different settings, run product through the machines and determine what combination of settings give the highest yields or the fewest defects. Without a designed program, it would otherwise take a very large number of trials to find a near optimum. I have often thought we should try to apply design of experiments to social situations.

In this example, I have limited the number of variables to four, showing it is impossible to juggle even a small number of variables with only two options. But in most real life situations, the number of variables can be in the hundreds or thousands and the options can cover continuous ranges. If it isn't obvious already, this is why "top-down" solutions never work. Because thoughts are liner and serial, they cannot solve the dynamic multi-variant and time dependent problems that we frequently encounter, such as global issues of society: religion, economics, politics, etc. To think otherwise is, in my opinion, sheer arrogance.

Historically, religious leaders have tried to think through these complex issues of life and death and arrive at grand conclusions. Doing so, the large numbers of religions have arrived at different conclusions. Thinking limitations are the Achilles-heels of top-down postulated systems.

Certainly thoughts and language can produce significant results. You can have serial thoughts, record them, add them to the thoughts of others, organize them, study them, reject the chaff, and arrive at complex thought patterns that form the basis of a hypothesis. But that doesn't get you to truth. The idea then has to be tested by experimentation and confirmation to arrive at tentative truth. This is the very basis of our human progress. Based on these observations, I doubt that any person or any religion can think or have thought their way to cosmic truths. So there goes all creeds and dogmas for me.

In this section, I have tried to show that thinking has limits.

This has not always been appreciated. Think of all the philosophers who have tried to think through the complexities of life. Think of the very different conclusions they have reached. It is amazing how many utopias have been proposed by individuals thinking they comprehended the big picture. Whether the big picture is about government, education, religion, social institutions, financial, or what-have-you, someone assumes he has thought through the perfect system or the ultimate truth. Short of designed experiments or pre-programmed algorithms, I doubt that thinking can reach optimum results. So take that, all you Republicans and Democrats! Ditto for priests and philosophers!

Our Small Window

We live in a very small window in the universe, and seldom stop to realize how precariously we are balanced with the necessities of life. By this I mean that there are extreme limits on our existence. If we get too much or too little oxygen, we cannot survive. If we get too much or too little radiation, we die. Even the slightest change to the earth's speed and gravitation and we are toast.

Many of our common measurement systems have utilitarian value within our window, but are only approximations. An easy example is time. Within our window, we universally measure time in seconds, minutes, hours, days, etc. But when a rocket is circling the earth at a faster speed than the earth is traveling, time stretches out.

Time slows down as either velocity or gravity increases. An astronaut traveling faster than the speed of earth will experience time slowing down. On the same flight, the higher he travels, the weaker the gravity, thus speeding up time. On balance, the combined effect results in a small slowing down of time. We joke about a modern day Rip Van Winkle who goes into space and returns to a world that has moved ahead much faster. At the present speed and altitude of space travel, the difference is very small. But the very thought that time is not consistent under all conditions is rather disturbing.

Or take space. We conveniently measure distance in inches, feet, yards, etc. We assume it is linear and this works well in our window. But outside our window, where does space terminate? It makes no sense to have it go on indefinitely in every direction. If space is not linear as we assume, but is actually curved, our measurements are only approximations. But they are very utilitarian in our small window.

Think of numbers. Within our window, we have a convenient, linear set of numbers: 1, 2, 3, 4 and so on to infinity. It's a useful system that we don't usually question because it is functional within our window. But just like space it boggles the imagination to think that it continues forever with no finish line. We really believe in finish lines. Infinity is just a word that suggests a termination where there really is none.

The great mathematician Kurt Gödel had something to say about this. He worked at the Advanced Institute in Princeton with the likes of Albert Einstein. In 1922 he published the now famous Gödel Theorem. He said that any postulated system that is complete is necessarily inconsistent, and conversely, any postulated system that is consistent is necessarily incomplete. The implications of this are enormous.

To illustrate this, think of a quilt. Along the top edge, list all the numbers from zero to infinity. Be complete and don't leave out any numbers. Now along the vertical edge, again list all the numbers from zero to infinity. Again be complete. Now fill in the rest of the quilt by continuing each column and row until the quilt is filled with numbers like a completed crossword puzzle.

If I asked you to count all the markings on the quilt, you would need more numbers than there are numbers because you carefully included all the numbers across each edge. Literally, there are more markings than there are numbers. But that can't be. You carefully included all the numbers along each axis. That means the system must be inconsistent. In fact, if you counted all the markings, you would need an infinity-squared number of numbers and that is impossible within our number system.

Now we have to think about the many postulated systems in our lives. Are our tax laws complete and consistent? Well, definitely not. Is our criminal code complete and consistent? Again no. Is our system of justice complete and consistent? Again, no. Are there any postulated systems that are complete and consistent? According to Gödel's Theorem, the answer is no. This undermines the postulated creedal system of every religion.

Which brings me back to the issue of church doctrine. Is it a postulated system that falls under the scrutiny of the Gödel Theorem? I think it is. It was unquestionably written by bishops after being hammered out at Nicaea and many subsequent councils. It is either complete or consistent, but not both and maybe neither. Does a postulated theology have any cosmic significance within our small window? On a larger scale, does a postulated theology have any relevance outside of our small window?

Another problem with any creed is that it is static. It resists change to retain its assumed authority over time. However it functions in a dynamic world that is constantly changing and undermining the tenets of a fixed creed.

Our religious forefathers believed that Earth was all of existence and naturally the center of creation. The stars circled Earth for man's benefit. With limited transportation, communication, tools like telescopes, their world was circumscribed. And I can empathize with their feeling of celestial importance.

Today, however, it is incredible to believe that our small window has any favorable position in the infinitely large universe with all we have learned about cosmology. There are now 1700 known planets circling stars and who knows if there is life on them. So much for theological privilege.

I see life on earth as being a very precarious reality that in no way is central to the importance of the cosmos. We exist with a delicate balance of factors and we resort to tools that are utilitarian and not universal in any sense. We understand enough to survive, but not enough to comprehend the mystery to which we were born. If Gödel was correct, which I believe he was, I think of all religions as postulated systems that cannot be both correct and consistent, probably neither.

Natural Laws

The natural laws are the most dependable things in our lives. They are consistent, invariant and impartial. They are the processes that govern everything. They are the foundational laws that regulate the dynamics of earth and everything on it. Weather obeys its laws as does chemistry and the optics in my vision. Nothing escapes these laws.

By natural laws, I refer to the ever-present concepts like gravity, refraction and capillary action. They always work dependably, consistently and impartially. If this were not so, scientists could not quantify their properties. And others could not confirm their findings with independent testing. Neither could engineers build products and structures without being able to depend on the properties of materials. And most probably, neither you nor I would go in for surgery or take an airplane flight without the absolute confidence that the properties of natural laws are repeatable and dependable.

It is good to have total confidence in something.

The beauty of nature, from forests to flowers and waterfalls, from sunsets to rainbows to snowflakes, are all by-products of the natural laws in action. These are not the majesty of a god, but the working out of natural systems. But so are the devastating tragedies of hurricanes, floods and wild fires. I believe the answer to the moral question of "Why do bad things happen to good people" is simply that the physical laws are impartial to our needs and wants.

If there is anything in this world that you can truly believe in, it is natural law. Everyone knows this and relies on the natural laws without much thought. They are so dependable that we take them for granted and they lose their drama until something unexpected happens, usually with the weather.

But the natural laws do not provide what many people desire. And that is something that is beyond nature, something that is supernatural and special for them. They may want a prayer answered, a quick fix for a problem or the assurance of life after death. These desires fall in the area of miracles, of things unseen but imagined and hoped for. As Julius Caesar once remarked: "As a rule, what is out of sight disturbs men's minds more seriously than what they see."

I still hear people talk about supernaturalism. I can understand the rise of supernaturalism at a time when our ancestors were looking for answers and didn't have the knowledge or tools to find them. But it is an idea that has long passed its time. There is absolutely nothing that transcends or violates natural law. To persist in citing supernaturalism in an age as advanced as ours is an educational travesty.

The problem is that you cannot have both natural laws and supernaturalism. Natural laws form a perfectly inter-related system of forces that are in dynamic balance. The violation of any one of the laws to accommodate a miracle would throw the entire system out of balance. For those who know anything about science, the altering of any part of a complex, inter-related system would have catastrophic consequences and we would not be able to put Humpty-Dumpty back together again.

What we do not see is any evidence of intervention by a god or supernatural forces that alters the laws of nature. Biblical stories like the parting of the Red Sea for Moses or stopping the sun for Joshua would require a god to intervene and invalidate his own natural laws. These "interruptions" just don't seem to happen in modern times. And that is why I accept such stories are more myths than miracles.

More to the point, no one has ever been able to change any natural law. And all the wishing in the world will not alter these laws. We should be thankful for our very survival that no one can tamper with them.

Among the most fascinating and complex manifestations of these natural laws are the properties of chemicals. They are the building blocks of all that exists: organic and inorganic. There are literally billions of combinations of these elements that make up all organic, plant and animal life. In one form or another, they form the foods that nourish us and the bacteria that kill us. The mosquito carrying the malaria virus is as natural a byproduct of the system as the cow that provides beef for our table. Again, we see the impartiality of the system.

Humans have some properties that are touchable and others that are un-touchable. This has supported the concept of a dualistic nature of body and soul since Rene Descartes proposed it: the one temporal and the other eternal. It fuels the ego that dreads the thought of death. It is hard for man to accept that combinations of chemical elements could produce intangibles such as consciousness, memory, intuition, feelings and anxiety. Now we know that all of the intangible properties are by-products of electro-chemical activities in our bodies. What an intriguing advancement in science! Now is the time to say goodbye to supernaturalism.

I am convinced that all life can be explained naturally and there are no supernatural forces. The tendency to explain unusual things by mystical or supernatural causes is a carryover from yester-year and slows the search for rational answers. Neither do I believe that there is a god who interferes with natural laws or intervenes in the lives of people. There is simply no evidence of this. Regardless how hard you pray for it not to rain on your wedding day or for your football team to win, it makes no difference. In WW II, the Germans and the Americans prayed to the same Christian god.

What makes freakish and unnatural experiences seem supernatural is the workings of different parts of our brain. The limbic system helps us stay close to reality. Its goal is our survival. It releases "feel good" chemicals that say "this is good for you, go for it." And it releases "feel bad" chemicals that say "this is bad for you, avoid it." The amygdala is also part of your survival system that interprets threats to you. But it can often over react. It can see a stick and think it is a snake or hear the floor creek and think there are intruders or ghosts. But worse of all is the neo-cortex. It can conceive totally imaginary things or retain parts of a dream upon waking.

How we combine these things is personal. It is a function of how the individual pathways of our brain have been soft-wired over our life. A true believer can take the least supportable of these inputs and elevate them to a supernatural event. A less susceptible person will choose the more probable route and look for a natural cause.

An easy example of this is the subject of illness. You can go to 100 doctors, ask their opinions, and get their judgments. Suppose 97 agree with one diagnosis and three suggest another. Well, I think a rational personal would go with the overwhelming majority of 97. But there are always people who would argue that the doctors are not 100% in agreement. They are giving more credence to the exceptions than to the high probability conclusion.

Many people use the "exceptions" to support their faith because it agrees with their mind-sets.

Evolution

I am fond of the two creation stories in chapters one and two of Genesis in the Old Testament. There is something significant about the early Hebrew writers including both of them. They certainly recognized the inconsistency in them. But they chose to put them side-by-side. Each version was written by a different person who was trying to explain the unexplainable issue of our origin. Certainly no witnesses were there. And God did not send different revelations to the two scribes. Including both versions of creation is a testimony that the compilers of the Book of Genesis knew that they were poetry, not history. There was no need to be consistent because their message was symbolic.

I admire those ancient writers. They were doing their best to answer complex questions for their people. They presented, each in their own way, a vision of creation that flowed logically and satisfied the needs of the times. I doubt that we could have done as well in those times.

However, in 1857, Charles Darwin moved the discussion from poetry to scientific inquiry. He gave evidence that all life evolved and continues to evolve by a process of natural selection.

This was achieved by exquisite observation, not experimentation. On a four-year trip to the Galapagos Islands, he noticed that there were numerous species of animals. The birds especially intrigued him. He noticed that the beaks of birds differed depending on the shape of the access to their food supplies. He reasoned that birds fortunate enough to have the proper shaped beaks to gain access to food survived and reproduced more easily than birds with different shaped beaks. He noticed that birds on different islands had different shaped beaks matched to the access of their food supply. He did not know the reason for this, but called it natural selection.

He collected an enormous number of species that he could study for small differences when he returned to England. And he studied them for years to confirm his initial observations.

He was very aware that sportsmen in England had bred animals for different characteristics. Dogs were bred for hunting, racing, and companionship. Pigeons were bred for homing, horses were bred for military skills and flowers were hybridized for special effects. Everyone knew that cross breeding produced new characteristics.

And he knew that fossils were being collected that showed variation among animals over time.

But what was natural selection? Darwin didn't know. It turned out to be nothing more than random mutations causing changes to the genes that were either advantageous or disadvantageous in the environment in which the species lived. Scientists now estimate that each person experiences about 35 mutations in his lifetime. The changes that are beneficial in the environment give a reproductive advantage and a higher probability that these mutated genes will thrive.

Darwin realized that such a process would take a very long time to produce the effects he had observed. He worried that the time span was too short. It was not until later estimates of the age of the earth were available, spanning billions of years, that he was convinced that evolution was possible.

Still, Darwin did not publish these ideas for a long time. He realized that if natural selection was true, it also applied to humans. His wife, Emma, was a conventional Christian who believed than man was made in the image of God, and if Charles persisted in such "foolery" he would be damned and they would not be together in eternity. He had actually sketched out his ideas in 1839, written a 35-page outline in 1842 and a 189-page manuscript in 1844 presenting his theory of evolution by natural selection. He left a note to Emma requesting that it be published after his death.

It was not until another scientist, Alfred Russel Wallace, came to the same conclusion that Darwin's friends convinced him to publish, knowing he had come up with the idea first. His book, *On The Origin of Species*, presenting the theory of evolution, was strongly opposed initially. And it still is in a few, but diminishing, circles. The Church has had a particularly hard time dealing with it. Over time, it has argued for Intelligent Design and Creationism as alternatives to evolution. But in every case, the courts have ruled that they are not science but religion and should not be taught. Even the Roman Catholic Church has finally accepted evolution, but with the twist that it is the means by which God operates.

On the negative side, politicians have abused the theory by creating Social Darwinism. They concluded that anyone who is weak should not be given help because they are inferior and should be left to die. The misapplication completely ignores the slow time dimension involved with evolution.

Today it is recognized as one of the three basic ideas in biology. Large numbers of Nobel Prize winners have signed petitions supporting the theory. John Gribbon in his excellent book *The Scientist* wrote: "In spite of all the other achievements of science in the nineteenth century, Darwin's and Wallace's achievement reigns supreme."

I am compelled by the accumulating evidence, and the support of the scientific community, to accept evolution as fact and to enjoy creation stories as cultural myths.

Jacques, Our Amazing Cat

At the time of this writing, my wife, Lee, has been in hospice for 20 months with congestive heart failure. I chose in-house hospice for her so we could be together. After all, we have been married for 47 years and I love her dearly. It has been somewhat confining to stay so close for so long. About eight months into this new lifestyle, I thought it would be a comfort for both of us to have a cat as a companion. Throughout our marriage we almost always had cats and we love their sense of aloof independence.

We have a wonderful friend, Gloria Kinney, who volunteers at the Buddy Foundation, a local animal shelter for strays. Her regular function is to go to the shelter at 6:00 AM on each Monday morning and feed 80 cats. But she is tender hearted and when a stray cat is pregnant, she takes it home because she cannot bear seeing the cat deliver her litter in a wire cage. Gloria has dedicated one of her bathrooms for the feline delivery room. It is furnished with soft rugs, food, water, cat toys, etc. When the litter is born, she cares for them for about ten weeks until they are old enough to be separated from their mother. Then she returns them to the shelter for adoption.

Occasionally, a mother cat will give birth to a kitten that is deformed in some way. Gloria realizes that if she returns the deformed cat to the shelter, it will not be adopted in preference to a cute, healthy cat. So she keeps them at her home.

At the time I was thinking about a cat, I was somewhat ambivalent. What if Lee and the cat did not relate well? What if I wanted to travel? Gloria came to the rescue. She offered to loan us a cat indefinitely that we could return at any time. She even delivered the cat to our home, complete with cat food, toys, bed, brushes, litter box and litter.

The cat was born to a mother with a French name, so all the litter were given French names. My loaner cat was named Jacques. He is a long hair, solid black and beautiful cat. His only defect is his left eye. He was born with a dry tear duct and his left eye never developed. That was fine with me. I have macular degeneration in my left eye and know what it means to function with one eye. We quickly became a pair of "one-eyed Jacques."

Jacques had been raised for about a year in Gloria's loving, caring home. When he came to us, he was a friendly, trusting and totally housebroken cat. He was not afraid of anyone. When friends come to visit, he approaches and greets them immediately. Within three months, Lee and I had become so attached to Jacques that we couldn't imagine being without him. I wrote Gloria a sincere thank you letter and told her how attached we were to Jacques. That is when she called back and said we could have him. And if I ever wanted to travel, she would be glad to "cat-sit" him. What a clever way to place so-called "disadvantaged" cats! Gloria is very clever as well as caring and loving.

Jacques' favorite toy is a multi-colored ribbon attached to a wand that a friend, Susan McCormick, gave him. When anyone dangles the ribbon, he jumps and tries to catch it. When he does, he proudly walks away with the ribbon in his mouth.

He loves to take walks. And he does not need any encouragement to do so. He is curious and investigates everything. He cherishes running down the hall at full speed. It is something to watch his little rump swaying back and forth as he runs. When Jacques and I go for a walk, I take the ribbon toy and wave it like a band conductor's baton. The point of this story is that Jacques learned to associate the ribbon toy with walking. He will lie down next to the ribbon toy hoping I will see him and understand he wants to walk. If I ignore his hints, he will drag the ribbon to me. And if I am in bed when he gets the urge, he will jump on the bed pulling the ribbon behind him, plastic wand and all.

Living with Jacques has been a wonderful experience. He is one smart cat. When I wash my face, he jumps on the lavatory counter and licks himself clean. When I work at the computer, he jumps on the desk and watches the cursor as I move the mouse. When I go to the toilet, he comes into the bathroom and gets in his litter box. When I take a nap, he takes – what else --a catnap. And when it's mealtime, he sits in the chair next to me and politely taps my knee with his paw, hoping I will slip him some food. He loves V-8 juice, cashew nuts, and especially peach yogurt.

I need no further demonstration than these to convince me that there is a functional brain in Jacques that learns, remembers, has feelings, is curious and loving. And I think that anyone who has had a loving pet would agree.

We know that evolution is conservative and reuses the same functional genes in many species. Scientists say that a mouse contains 90 percent of the same genes that humans do and chimpanzees, our closest animal relative, contain 98.5%. I don't know how many genes Jacques and I share, but he is smarter than any mouse and I would put him up against a chimpanzee in any contest except swinging from trees. I can almost hear him say: "Who needs opposing thumbs when you have opposing jaws!"

From my close relation with Jacques, I cannot agree with the church doctrine that man is made in the image of God and has dominion over all the animals and the earth. First it would be an insult to God to think that he looks anything like me or has the mentality of our politicians. Second, I think man has been irresponsible in managing nature with the selfish result of polluting the air and waters, strip mining the land, and deforesting the trees. The Indians did a much better job revering Mother Earth. Third, I do not see mankind and animals as dualistic opposites. I see all life existing on a continuum with a high level of genetic commonality and evolutionary history, some species being very smart and all being selectively adapted to their environments.

P.S. I wish everyone gave me as much pleasure as Jacques does.

DNA: Our Genetic Lifeline

When I chose the title *From God to DNA* for this book, I was not trying to be facetious or stimulate sales. The title reflects a real transition in my life. To my knowledge, DNA is the only thing that can create life. And since it moves from one generation to the next in an unbroken line, it is the only thing I know that approaches immortality and sweeps a small bit of each of us into the future. Do I remember Jesus saying that the Kingdom of God is within you?

When I was very young, I was taught that God was all loving, all knowing and all powerful. I was taught that he answered prayers and interceded in the lives of his children. But I don't see any evidence of this. We are familiar with all too many atrocities like war, famine and disease that beg the question: "Why doesn't God intervene? Where is this loving, caring Father?"

We were told that God was the ultimate answer to the most pressing human questions. But it seems to be an answer endlessly delayed. During my studies I have slowly seen God evaporate before my eyes. I find nothing behind the word God that is worth putting my faith and trust in anymore. Gods are the graveyards of hope.

By contrast, I have found something that truly is answering questions for me. These are the same questions that I used to ask of God and got no answers. During the last half century, the scientific world has opened up explanations about the workings of the human genome, especially the brain, that I find amazing. I have followed this scientific effort as best I can as an amateur and find myself fascinated beyond measure. What I like most is the promise of DNA to understand and help cure people with illnesses that religion can't touch.

I recognize that many people are not familiar with the advances of modern neuroscience and cannot appreciate the contrast I am making here. I strongly urge you to start reading. It is truly the leading edge of science and self-understanding.

Now that we have moved from the section on God to the section on DNA, I owe it to the reader to explain the title in more detail. For this, I am going to back up a few billion years and witness the beginning of life itself.

••••••••••••••

The most common elements on the planet in the pre-historic era were carbon, hydrogen, oxygen and nitrogen, collective known by the acronym CHON. These elements were not unique to Earth, but were the result of exploding stars that spread throughout the Universe.

Combinations of these elements are known to make amino acids, the building blocks of all life. Dr. Harold Urey, Nobel Laureate, and a graduate student demonstrated in the laboratory how amino acids could be made quite easily. They put the four CHON gases into a flask, discharged an electrical spark through them, and discovered that they had produced an amino acid. This was a major scientific finding.

Obviously, if this could be done in a lab, it could be done naturally by lightening strikes on a much larger scale. And more lightening strikes with different concentrations of the same four CHON gases could produce different amino acids. We now know that only four different small amino acids are used in making DNA. They are called adenine (A), thymine (T), cytosine (C) and guanine (G).

What is fascinating to me is how these small amino acids couple together. When two amino acids join, they do not necessarily stay in a flat plane. Each of them has positive or negative charges that attract or repel adjacent parts, causing them to fold. When a third amino acid joins the first two, there is more folding. This process continues until they form structures that are very modernistic. The smallest gene contains about 300 co-joined amino acids and looks like a bowl of spaghetti.

The important concept here is that the shape determines its function. If any one of the basic acids, A, T, C, or G, is accidently substituted for another in transcription at any location in the "chain", it will result in an entirely different shape, hence function. By function, I mean what it does in the body, like being a muscle cell, a liver cell, etc. These complex shapes form receptor sites such that specific chemicals can communicate with them.

Progressively these small amino acids coupled together to make more complex molecules that would eventually grow to become our enormous DNA.

From early on, these molecules exhibited behaviors that implied they had a mission and a strategy for achieving it. The mission has three parts that have never changed. They (1) adapt to the environment, (2) survive and (3) reproduce. In a curious way, this evolving molecule seems to be creative. But I know that it is just adjusting to the environment in a way that allows it to survive. Think of these remarkable adaptations.

Certain advantageous mutations allowed it to extract energy from the environment by a process we call photosynthesis. It evolved a respiratory system that allowed it to survive in the presence of toxic oxygen. It evolved systems of metabolism to process food and extract its nutrients. All the while it was getting bigger and forming new species by mutations.

I don't know when the intangible qualities entered in this progressive growth. We certainly know that we possess thinking, feelings and morals. We see smaller animals that also possess at least some of these qualities. And we can reasonably assume that they did not appear fully developed like fireworks on the Fourth of July. For example, it is known that before these evolving life forms evolved pigmentation, members of their colony would crawl on top of others and sacrifice themselves to protect the colony from harmful radiation, all in the name of survival. Was there thinking or morality there?

They evolved appendences in the forms of fins, wings and

legs to obtain locomotion. They evolved all the senses to let them communicate with the outside world for survival. The list goes on and on to include every feature and function of every species. But most impressive of all, for me, is the evolution of the human brain.

There is evidence that the human brain evolved in three stages. The earliest part was called the reptilian brain. It is found in very early life forms and has been retained by us through evolution. It controls most of the automatic functions of the body. The second part of the brain to develop was the limbic system that controls most of the emotions of the body. It is the first part of the brain to receive sensory information and to take action on it quickly for our protection. The third part to develop was the neo-cortex that is used for executive functions, judgments, analysis, etc. The limbic system is faster than the neo-cortex and often over-rides judgment in taking actions. The rule of counting to ten before taking any action makes neurological sense.

And all this "growth" was done by billions and billions of beneficial mutations. Of course, there were billions and billions of non-beneficial mutations that caused some species to be less adaptive to the environment and eventually reproduce less and die off. Mutations are amoral. If they aid the species, all is well and good. If they don't, it's the cruel price of progress. Like all natural laws, they are impartial.

This process would not be thinkable without the billions of years that the process has been going on. But now we know that the mechanism of natural selection that enables evolution is the mutation of genes. And the collective result of all advantageous mutations is the molecule of life known as DNA.

I find this incredible. It boggles my mind to learn that something that has been shrouded in mystery is finally revealing itself through patient research.

And it stands to reason that the process continues. The DNA molecule will continue to grow in size and complexity and mankind will evolve with it to higher levels of humanism. Some day we may even be able to solve differences without violence.

As early as the 1940s, Alfred Hershey and Martha Chase proved that the genetic material of viruses is composed of DNA. DNA is a shorthand symbol for the extremely complex molecule deoxyribonucleic acid. Since all life derives from this same molecule, DNA is now known to be the organic substance carrying the human genome.

By 1952, Rosalind Franklin, using X-ray diffraction, showed that the DNA molecule had a double-helix structure.

Using this as a starting point, James Watson and Francis Crick conceived of a model in 1953 that consists of two rails like the sides of a ladder but spiraling like a barber's pole, 180 degrees out of phase with each other. Connecting to the rails like the rungs of a ladder were pairs of those original four small amino acids mentioned earlier: adenine (A), thymine (T), cytosine (C) and guanine (G). Each pair is called a base. But the exact arrangement was not known.

It was left for the mathematician John Griffith to figure out that when an A was coupled to a T through a double hydrogen bond and a C was coupled to a G through a triple hydrogen bond that the pairs were the same length. This would make either an A-T pair or a C-G pair fit as rungs in the spiral ladder. We now know that an A will only bond to a T and a C will only bond to a G.

When you put these ideas together, you get a DNA model with two spiraling rails called a double helix. When an A is attached to one rail, a T will be attached to the opposite rail connected by a weak double hydrogen bond. And when a C is attached to the first rail, a G will be attached to the second also connected by its triple hydrogen bond. This makes the A-T and C-G nucleotide pairs look like ladder rungs. The resulting DNA molecule resembles a very long spiral staircase, estimated to have 3.2 million nucleotide pairs or rungs.

The Nobel Prize for this achievement was awarded to Watson, Crick and Wilkins in 1962. Rosalind Franklin was not included because she had died of cancer in 1958. However, Maurice Wilkins, her supervisor of the work, was included.

Now that the DNA **structure** was known, it was necessary to identify the **genetic code** that produces all of the chemistry of life that permits survival, adaptation and reproduction. Since there are 20 and arguably 21 essential amino acids needed for life, they require a code that produces at least 21 combinations. However, four nucleotide bases (A, T, C, & G) taken 2 at a time would produce only 16 combinations and would not satisfy the condition. Therefore, the four nucleotide bases would have to be taken three at a time and form an excessive number of 64 combinations to satisfy the requirement. Three adjacent bases taken together are called a codon and is the basic alphabet of the genetic code.

Hundreds or even thousands of codons are required to form a gene, the basic unit of heredity. There are approximately 22,500 genes in the human. All of these genes are located on one of the 23 pairs of chromosomes. Genes make proteins and in various combination, they are capable of making at least 250,000 different proteins. Finally, proteins make cells, the building blocks of life. In a cell, there are about 20,000 proteins and each cell has a nucleus that has a complete copy of the DNA with which it can make additional proteins as needed. We are dealing here in the world of the ultra small.

Only 20% of genes code for proteins. In the early days, researchers called the remainder "junk" genes. We now know that these are not the kind of junk you put in the garbage, but the kind of junk you put in the attic for later use.

Some of these "junk" genes function as timekeepers. There are critical periods when you are more sensitive to learning a subject. There is a time delay before puberty sets in. The neo-cortex of the brain continues to grow until you are about 21 years old, long past those risk-taking teenage years. Some regulatory genes have to turn these functions on and off. And others have to tell them when.

There are placement genes known as Hox genes that tell where the arms are to be located on the body, where the legs are, where the nose is, and so forth. All this requires information and a plan.

There are repair mechanism genes that are idle until they are needed and signaling genes to inform them where they are needed.

There are immune system genes that can identify a foreign substance and destroy it. But these genes have to be smart enough not to attack a human fetus that is an unfamiliar substance. This is why a cancer cell can evade the immune system; it is only a mutation of a normal cell.

If this isn't impressive enough, the DNA completely renews itself every two months and rebuilds the skin every month, the liver every six weeks, the stomach every five days, the bones every three months, the blood every four months and the brain once a year.

The genome not only carries functioning genes, it also carries pseudo-genes, genes that were previously used for body hair, tails, etc. These genes are considered to be "broken," but every now and then, a child will be born with an ancestral part that has to be removed. The genome is more than a current gene index. It is more like a history book of all genes past and present.

Mistakes in transcribing DNA (copying errors in DNA) are not frequent, but it does happen. Further, genes can be mutated by a number of environmental factors like radiation and free radicals. These infrequent occurrences are all that Darwinian evolution needs to explain natural selection.

This is hard for some people to accept. There are so many forms of life and each has such unbelievable complexity. Yet each evolved from the same start. The number of genes that are common to various species is remarkable. We contain 98.5 percent of the same genes as the chimpanzee. So scientists can do research on mice, flies, monkeys and snails knowing that the results apply to humans. Yes, flies get drunk on alcohol and become aggressive.

Assuming the number of 22,500 genes in a human and only 1.5% are different from chimpanzees, there are less than 350 genes that makes us different. Major research is being done to determine what these select genes do. Here are some examples.

Scientists say that the ASPM gene regulates the number of times the neuronal stem cells divide. In the chimpanzee it divides once; but in the human it divides three times giving us a much larger brain.

The FOXP2 gene regulates the size of the jaw muscle. In apes it creates large jaw muscles to help crack nuts and other raw foods. But in the human a mutation has caused the jaw muscle to be small, allowing more room for a larger skull, hence brain, and still pass through the birth canal. The smaller jaw muscles are more flexible for synthesizing speech.

The SRY gene determines manliness. The EDAR gene plays a role in the development of hair, teeth and sweat glands. The Paxb gene causes development of the eye. And the SRGAP2 gene causes neurons to have complex shapes capable of exchanging information with neighboring cells. These are only six of the 22,500 genes we have and each has an equivalent special function to perform.

These examples are illustrative and bring us to the really important point. The genes, of necessity, carry specific information and the ability to act on it. There is an incredible amount of information in the DNA needed to produce and sustain life. It is just amazing how this electro-chemical molecule does all it does. And we take it for granted.

Knowing the DNA structure and the genetic code, now let's look at the principal goals of the human genome. Recall the three basic strategies: survival, reproduction and adaptation to the changing environment. In carrying out these functions, it passes this information to the next generation and the next. It is the only thing that approaches immortality

The DNA strategy for survival is to provide you with a large number of chemicals -- neurotransmitters and hormones -- that singularly or collectively produce all your feelings. The behaviors that help you survive are accompanied with the release of chemicals that produce positive feelings like anticipation, pleasure and status. The behaviors that could endanger your survival are accompanied by the release of chemicals that produce painful feelings and caution you to take action.

The DNA strategy for reproduction is to get you to be a partner in its selfish goal of continuity. We are like pawns in the DNA's game to get to the next generation and the next and the next. DNA cannot do this without us. So it makes us willing pawns with a sub-strategy of making love, sex, children and family pleasurable. We willingly carry out the DNA's strategy for the pleasure it provides.

Survival and reproduction are easy to understand. As proof,

there is an unbroken chain of survival and reproduction that allows us to exist today.

What is difficult for many to appreciate is that the genes are constantly sampling the environment to adapt to changing conditions. On a physical basis, there is no question that the air we breathe, the fluids we drink, and the foods we eat are vastly different over the short span of a few centuries. The genetic code continues to take advantage of positive mutations to respond to these changes.

Unquestionably this process continues. We are routinely confronted with harmful mutations that lead to medical disorders like cancer. And we are cautioned to take anti-oxidants to reduce the effect of free radicals. Of course, we are thinking about the negative mutations.

But there are positive mutations that are conditioning us for the changing environment we live in. And they apply to our societal world. We no longer live in the essential isolation of the long ago past. The threats to our survival are no longer limited to wild life, food shortages and extreme weather. Today, most of us live in highly populated areas and there are many new threats to our collective survival. With population increasing worldwide, industrials pollutants, potentially limited water, fuel and food supplies, with climate changes, religions that resort to terrorism, and governments that cannot agree in a thermonuclear age, there are serious threats to our joint survival. We depend on the services of others and most of us are no longer self-sufficient. We benefit from shared knowledge, medical help, food supplies, auto repairs, etc. We may reproduce individually, but we survive collectively. And I like it that way.

How would one expect the DNA to beneficially adapt as our environment is changing? How would it maximize its chance of survival and reproduction?

Well, part of the answer is known. The DNA has evolved mirror neurons that allow us to relate to the problems of others. When we see someone in pain, we feel empathy and sympathy. We share in their distress and want to help. We see this in very young children before they have been taught about morality. If one child expresses pain, another will try to comfort him. In a collective society with common threats, we are truly in this together.

As I said before, our internal moral code is very probably an epiphenomenon of the genetic code. By this I mean that true morality is not a cultural happenstance, but a result of our genes responding to the needs of joint survival for their own survival and reproduction. It is beyond coincidence that something like the Golden Rule appeared in every culture and every religion at essentially the same time. It is certainly not in the gene's reproductive interest for us to kill each other, either individually or collectively. That is why I can argue that the genes may be adapting to accommodate both individual and joint survival.

That takes me to the issue of consciousness. No one knows, yet, why we have consciousness or awareness. Until a better answer is found, I hold that the same gene structure has made us aware of ourselves so we can see and understand how we relate to others. Again, it is in the gene's benefit for us to discipline ourselves for joint survival.

It is rather scary to think that the DNA is an inanimate chemical structure that contains the information to produce a life, manage its growth, automate its regulation, adapt to the environment, and, above all, orchestrate a dynamic, flexible strategy for survival that anticipates your life situations before you do and chemically provides the appropriate feelings.

For me it is dumb-founding to imagine all of the information that is encoded chemically in the DNA and executed routinely to produce life out of inorganic materials. If there is anything I call miraculous, surely it is this life producing and enhancing force. And yes, I am beginning to have reverent feelings about this.

When I was young, I was told that I was created by God in His image. This explanation does not allow for the dynamic evolving of all life forms. Only evolution using the mechanism of natural selection with mutations of the DNA can explain what we have learned about life.

Do you begin to see why my allegiance has shifted from God,

our cultural wish, to DNA, the tangible and increasingly explainable cause of the miracles of life? Or is this the God incarnate implied in Jesus' words that the Kingdom of God in within you?

Once I overcame the brain-numbing, irrational repetition of ancient mystical beliefs in churches and realized that supernaturalism cannot possibly co-exist with a system of interconnected natural laws, I could move into modernity. The last remaining hurdle for me – and probably for most people – was to surrender the ego-satisfying, existential hope for life after death. Without this, progress is handicapped with the drag of ancient religious mysticism.

With this understanding, I do not believe that I was created by God in His image or have any allegiance to a supernatural figure. I believe that all animal life is a result of evolution and the mechanism for this progressive development is the information in the DNA molecule that is forever adapting to its environment and growing in complexity.

Finally, I want to give praise to Francis Crick who was instrumental in determining both the structure and the genetic code of the DNA. It was his life's mission from 1953 to his death in 2004. The enormity of this contribution to our understanding and our future is overwhelming. The fame of Crick ranks with Copernicus, Newton, Darwin and Einstein as the leading conceptual scientists of all time.

Neuroscience

We really haven't finished talking about DNA. This unbelievably complex molecule carries the information that builds every organ in our bodies. Of those organs, the brain is considered to be the most complex organ in the Universe. For me, it is hard to think that the brain as more complex than the DNA that makes it.

Neuroscience is the study of the brain and how it functions. Evolving an organism as complex as the brain over millions of years is one thing; understanding it in real time is quite another. Today there are over 100,000 neuroscientists in many major universities and industrial labs around the world trying to unravel this, one of the greatest challenges.

I grew up in a time when answers to ephemeral concepts like memory, thinking, awareness, and consciousness, were beyond our rational ability. We knew they existed, but we had no explanations except to resort to mystical answers. Some were satisfied to call this soul, but others were not. As I said, to give something a name is not to know it and, particularly, not to understand it.

We know we are not plugged into electrical outlets. Nor do we run on batteries. The miracle of our being is enabled by a self-contained, electro-chemical system specified and maintained by the DNA's human genome. Our genome is a huge collection of amino acids that code everything that is needed for life. It is information that goes into action with directions for all bodily functions, regulations, repairs, immune suppression, developmental critical periods, in short, everything.

I am certainly not a neuroscientist, but if had my career to do over again, I would be. This is truly the leading edge of science, trying to answer the questions that have puzzled mankind through the ages. I do have an enormous interest in the subject and have been facilitating a course to learn the jargon so we can read and basically understand new material as it is published.

It was not until the last century that science had the instrumentation, experimental procedures and collective understanding to begin explaining many of the sticky issues that have puzzled mankind's best philosophers and theologians. And we will need even better tools to keep the process going.

Much progress has been made. The evolving understanding of DNA has contributed significantly to the understanding of the brain. What we can safely say is that the mind is the functioning of the brain. When any part of the physical brain is damaged or diseased, the relevant function of the mind goes with it.

The brain is an electro-chemical organism. It has an amazing 85 billion brain cells called neurons. At the input side of the neuron are dendrites that resemble the branching top of a tree and receive inputs from other neurons. In the center on the neuron is the nucleus carrying the DNA with which it can make new proteins, essential for building memory. On the output side is a long member, like the taproot of a tree, called an axon. On the terminal end of the axon are many synapses that relate to the dendrites of the downstream neuron for signaling. Only a few of the neurons are hard-wired together. Most of the neurons are soft-wired and communicate with each other through many synapses, which are microscopically small gaps between the axon and the downstream dendrite. There are over 100,000 miles of these axons fibers that transmit signals to other parts of the brain and to muscles.

When an electrical action potential is generated in a neuron by up-stream inputs, it causes a chemical neurotransmitter to jump the synaptic gap and become an input to the down-stream neuron. It is estimated that each neuron has about 1200 synapses forming trillions of synaptic gaps. When a neuronal pathway is used more and more the number of synapses can easily double.

I must confess that I have trouble getting my mind around the complexity of all these billions of neurons forming interconnections and setting up an unthinkable number of alternative pathways. It is staggering.

There are presently reported to be about 50 neurotransmitters that either stimulate or inhibit neurons. Some of the better-known ones are glutamate that excites neurons and GABA that inhibits them. Here comes the unbelievable part. There are individual neurotransmitters that relate to each of our feelings. And all of them are part of the gene's survival mechanism in our limbic system, the emotional control system.

There is an interesting book by Loretta Breuning called *Meet Your Happy Chemicals.* She has simplified the language of neurotransmitters and I have abstracted the following passage from her book (hoping you will buy and read the whole book.)

"Happy chemicals are controlled by tiny brain structures that all mammals have in common: the hippocampus, amygdala, pituitary, hypothalamus, and other parts collectively known as the limbic system....Your limbic system releases neurotransmitters that tell your body "this is good for you, go towards it," and "this is bad for you, avoid it."....Your brain rewards you with good feelings when you do something good for your survival. Each of the happy chemicals motivates a different type of survival behavior. Dopamine motivates you to get what you need, even when it takes lots of effort. Endorphin motivates you to ignore pain so you can escape from harm when you're injured. Oxytocin motivates you to trust others, to find safety in companionship. And serotonin motivates you to get respect, which expands your mating opportunities and protects your offspring.... The mammal brain motivates a body to go toward things that trigger happy chemicals, and avoid things that trigger unhappy chemicals.... Bad feelings are produced by cortisol....When you feel a cortisol alert, your brain looks for a way to make it stop....Such feelings keep commanding your attention with the sense that you must "do something."...Your brain keeps scanning the world for a way to make bad feelings stop"

In addition, there are families of hormones produced in glands that are released into the blood stream, hormones like male testosterone and female estrogen. There are thousands of enzymes that react with foods as part of our metabolism. There are catalysts that speed up chemical reactions without entering into the process. Add in the neurotransmitters and you have the collection of chemicals that produces every feeling, thought or function we have: fear, love, anxiety, angst, compassion, greed, justice, etc., as well as all the motions we have like walking, moving, breathing, digesting, etc. There is no other source that could give rise to them. It's fun to think that we eat hamburgers and French fries, and our body chemistry somehow converts them into consciousness, feelings, thinking and memories. Not bad for a chemistry set.

To service the neurons, there are somewhere between three and ten times as many glial cells as neurons in the brain. There are three types of glial cells that protect, nourish and remove waste. The brain contains over 100,000 miles of blood vessels to feed it. Although the brain is only 2% of our body weight, it consumes about 25% of the total body energy.

The neurons are prolific communicators. They signal each other in combinations that elicit all the functions of life. This involves learning, storing and recalling memory, feelings, consciousness, emotions and everything else. Everything you have ever experienced and all the unconscious acts of regulating the body functions that you don't feel are controlled by the brain.

Further, this chemistry set has no instruction manual. It is a good thing that it knows what to do and is self- regulating. If we had to take control of regulating all the functions in our body we would die within minutes.

Neurological studies fall into two categories: Basic research and applied research.

The fundamental goal of basic research is to understand the molecular basis of our senses and emotions. The largest amount of research has gone into understanding how our vision works. We do not see color or complete pictures. Various cells detect different wavelengths reflected off of objects that we interpret as colors and aspects of a scene such as transitions, lines, brightness, singularities, etc. Only about 10% of this information is transmitted to the brain for interpretation. These elements of the visual field are stored in different visual cortices in the brain and reassembled when called to memory. Each time they are recalled, the image may not be exactly the same depending on how well and how frequently the individual elements are restored and recalled.

The Nobel Prize winner Eric Kandel has spent his entire career trying to understand the molecular basis of memory. His book, *In Search of Memory,* is a delightful and easy-to-read explanation of how the chemistry of the brain forms working memory that lasts for a few seconds, short-term memory that lasts a few days and long-term memory that lasts for long periods.

The goal of applied research is to use what we know to help people with mental and physical problems. Since using humans as subjects for study is not ethical, most researchers use animals that have a large genetic commonality with humans. Some scientists approach the subject from the perspective of understanding and potentially curing diseases like Parkinson's, depression, anxiety or OCD. Others study patients who have had accidents or strokes to see what functions are lost.

It is mind-boggling to read what they have learned. Researchers now know that the lack of dopamine is associated with Parkinson's disease, affecting memory and navigation. They know that when a span of 25 genes on the 6th chromosome is under-expressed it causes low social interaction found in autism and when it is over-expressed it causes hyper social mannerisms associated with Williams' Syndrome. The hormone oxytocin in mother's milk causes bonding with the child during nursing. The midbrain amygdala responds to threats and reacts before we can think about it. It also releases cortisol that produces stress. But when oxytocin is released, it quiets the amygdala and results in a feeling of trust.

Over the last 30 years, the endogenous reward system has found the pathways and chemicals that result in feelings of desire, drive, love, euphoria and religious ecstasy. The rewards can be so great that it can lead to addiction for anything from sex to recreational drugs.

I could go on and on, but I think this makes the point that there is an electro-chemical action that produces every aspect of our being, both tangible and intangible.

This is not intended to be a tutorial on the brain, but to provide a few examples of how our body chemistry creates those previously imponderable things like feelings of love, trust, desire, and fear. Slowly the parts are coming together. There is much to be done and understood. But we are close enough that the British and US governments have proposed separate ten-year programs for mapping the mind. This is similar to the earlier program of mapping the human genome that was a huge success and has returned $140 for each dollar spent.

It is obvious that I am amazed by the ability of the DNA to make and operate a brain. I can understand and appreciate how my forefathers had to struggle to deal with these gossamer concepts. I do not fault them for thinking they were mystical. But with the advance of science, I am equally convinced that such intangible functions are simply the workings of the brain. And with time we will know more details.'

In closing, let me speculate on a few of the imponderables of my youth such as memory recall, thinking and having thoughts. We know that television and a number of personal communicating devices produce pictures by streaming a large number of pixels in a controlled array. We also know the brain stores an enormous amount of information from the past to the present. Lastly, we know that a neuron is a binary cell that is either on or off. It doesn't seem like much of a stretch to think of memory recall, thinking, having thoughts, dreaming, inventing, hallucinating, etc, as selectively engaging memory pixels from various parts of memory storage and presenting them on the equivalent of a screen in the brain. I know that Francis Crick was looking for such a screen at the time of his death. And as for consciousness, I speculate it is just another sense. Just like we have five senses to sample the outside world, I think we have consciousness as a means to sample the inside world. Remember, this is speculation, but it begins to make more sense to propose some models that to have these ephemeral ideas free floating with no anchor.

Brain Plasticity

You may have guessed it, but we are still talking about another aspect of the DNA. Our DNA has given us brains with the quality of plasticity. This simply means that it is pliable and can be molded to accommodate newness, either physical or mental.

There is an interesting contrast between the plasticity that we have and the instincts of many animals. You can raise 50 generations of mice in a wire cage but when you put the 51st generation mouse on the ground for the first time, it will dig a borrow exactly like his distant ancestors. Other animals can walk almost immediately after they are born. They have hard-wired instincts, but we have mostly soft-wired plasticity.

One of the most remarkable advances in modern science is the understanding of this plasticity. For years, it was thought that the brain was fixed. In the 18th century the neo-cortex was mapped into a large number of regions and each was thought to be dedicated to a specific function of the body. This turns out to be only partially true. Now we know it is very pliable.

This should have been self-evident for most of us. We learn. We develop skills. And the only way we can achieve these things is by progressively re-structuring the brain to develop stronger pathways for the things we regularly think and do.

From the beginning, when a child experiences something that is pleasant, a squirt of dopamine will establish a pathway about that subject and remember it as being good. Good means it supports survival. The experience might be cuddling with the mother. The next time the child is cuddled and it feels good again, another squirt of dopamine will reinforce the original pathway and make it stronger.

When the child goes berry picking with her father, she will look at his face to see if he if smiling or frowning. If he is smiling, the child will release a squirt of dopamine (reward) and build a neuronal pathway around the pleasure of berries. When she later eats the berries with her cereal, she will have another pleasant experience and get another squirt of dopamine reinforcing the berry pathway.

When a child is complemented for anything done well, like putting up her toys, making good grades or practicing the violin, she will get a squirt of serotonin (status) that builds pathways of self- esteem and confidence.

Conversely, when the child touches a hot stove, she will experience pain and a squirt of cortisol will establish an avoidance pathway. Pain means it does not support survival.

Survival in this context does not refer to life-or-death situations. It refers to behaviors that enhance or jeopardize life on a small scale, leading collectively to one's long-term survival.

In the course of a day, a child can have tens or hundreds of emotional experiences including waking up, feeling rested, selecting clothes, tasting foods, having fun, playing, socializing with others, being criticized for not behaving, resisting taking a nap, petting the animals, falling and skinning a knee, experiencing mother's kiss to make it well, etc. Each experience builds or enforces pathways. In the course of childhood this grows to an enormous number of unique pathways for each child.

So a child grows up building Approach-Avoidance pathways depending on the unique experiences in his life. What he is doing is mapping his world to survive in the environment he grew up in. And although each of us has the same DNA to create the brain, it is our reactions to life experiences coupled with our genetic temperament that shape our individual personalities.

This is a good place to pause and express my amazement at this process. In our language we typically use the words feelings and emotions interchangeably. But in neuroscience, they do not. Feelings are what you experience. Emotions are what the unconscious "inner wisdom" of the body senses first to initiate your feelings. Emotion stems from emote, conveying start motion. It initiates feelings before you feel them.

Think about this: the brain senses the survival quality of something you anticipate doing, releases one of the 50 neurotransmitters or combinations thereof, and subsequently you experience the feeling. Likewise, the brain senses what you anticipate doing and sends signals from the motor cortex to the muscles before you can move. The DNA puppeteer is pulling all of the strings that give rise to your feelings and motions before you know about them. This is sort of scary. But it is also remarkable that a complex electro-chemical system can create and operate a control system that enhances the survival of both you and the DNA.

The brain's plasticity relates to the environment in yet another way. Some genes are methylated so they can't produce proteins. For example, you would not want the DNA in a brain nucleus to produce a liver protein. However, in adapting to the environment, the body has the ability to activate a needed gene by removing its methylation. So the brain is changing plastically to your experiences and to the environment, both for your long-term survival.

A pathway is the number of synapses that fire in response to a given sensation. The more we think the same thoughts or do the same things, the more synapses will be developed and the stronger those neuronal pathways become. It is not unusual for the number of synapses to expand from 1200 to 2700 on a single axon. In short, neurons that fire together wire together and are the basis of memory, habits, and personality.

Conversely, neurons that are not used will be eliminated. There is a protein C1p that marks neurons that are infrequently used. The microglia will destroy those marked neurons. An example of this relates to hearing. We are born with a set of about 50 types of hearing neurons for all possible phonetic sounds. A Japanese baby will never hear the sound of "r" spoken in his native language. With time the baby will lose the neuron associated with that sound. He will not be able to pronounce anything with an "r" in it. Instead of saying fried rice, he will say flied lice.

Of course, the environment that the adult lives in could be very different from the environment that the child grew up in. And the survival pathways (personality traits) that are developed as a child may be poorly suited for his adult needs. Parents tend to cater to their children in ways that are seldom repeated in marriage or business.

Fortunately, the plastic brain can create new pathways with deliberate practice. But it is easier to form new pathways than to change existing strong pathways that have grown into superhighways.

The neuroscientist of the last 70-years – more or less – have pushed the limits of plasticity. In the extreme, doctors can often get stroke victims to regain the use of disabled limbs. For example, each limb is associated with a part of the motor cortex. If that part of the cortex is damaged, it produces no signal to move the limb. However. if you manually move the limb using extensive physical therapy (therapy on steroids so to speak) the adjacent parts of the motor cortex on both sides of the damaged part will encroach and take over. And the patient will regain some use of the limb. The neurons have a great competition for space, oxygen and sucrose. Amazing.

One of my favorite books on the subject of brain plasticity is *The Brain That Changes Itself* by Norman Doidge, published in 2007. It presents case after case of patients who have experienced remarkable improvements by doctors manipulating the plasticity of the brain.

The brain is really a learning machine. It wants to learn. In fact, it is constantly learning ways to learn better. We have repeatedly said that one of the gene's basic functions is to adapt to the environment in which it lives. To adapt, the genes of the body must be in contact with the environment. For example, if you drink milk (an environmental item) and the body does not have enough of the enzyme lactase to process the milk's sugar lactose, it will make more immediately. This means that the brain is the mechanism that is sampling the environment to adapt, plastically, to new changes. And we all know the environment is constantly changing and we must be changing too.

Never forget that the gene's primary goal is survival. So the brain is constantly scanning the environment and adapting to it. Also, don't be fooled into thinking that your feelings are for your pleasure. They are all part of the gene's strategy for your survival. It's strategy is to make things pleasant when they are good for you, like eating when you are hungry, and unpleasant when they are bad for you, like over eating.

The brain needs regular exercise just like the body does. When a child is young and everything is new and novel, the brain is at its peak of absorbing new inputs and modeling the child's world. Not only is the child absorbing the most information, the brain is in its healthiest and functionally best state.

As we age, we settle into unchanging patterns. We accept one culture, one denomination, one political party, one diet, one daily routine, one group of friends, one attitude about money and we live in our personal comfort zones. We do not see the need to change things, whether they are working for us or not. When we fail at something, we simply try harder using the same beliefs and habits. They seem so natural you can almost hear people say: this is who I am, the summation of my life experiences. This is true up until now. But it won't be true tomorrow if you have experiences that can change you. You don't want to play tomorrow's game with yesterday's rules. And if you are not having new experiences, you should turn off the TV, get off the couch and seek out something new to exercise your brain and jolt your comfort levels.

It is easy to see how different cultural and religious concepts that are repeated over-and-over from infancy become internalized and believed. It is simply part of people's "soft-wiring" of the brain. If you also associate these concepts with values, they become noble and sacred. People will double down to support them although they may not be beneficial for them.

When I travel and relate to people of different cultures, I observed that parents generally wanted the same things for their children. Out of some common human core of wisdom, they want their children to be polite, to be educated, to learn some skill, to be good and to make something of themselves. This tends to be universal.

Yet when you look at the cultural and religious dressings, they vary so differently. The arbitrariness of these beliefs is easy to see when you travel among different cultures, or when immigrants bring different cultures to our doorsteps. It implies that we have a universal genetic core of values upon which we drape arbitrary cultural mores and religions. And since the mind is plastic, these "accessories" can gain dominance. On the other hand, exactly because the brain is plastic, any cultural "accessory" can be challenged and replaced by thinking new thoughts.

Living with closed opinions causes the human brain to suffer. With fixed beliefs and habits, there is less and less chance for the brain to be challenged and exercised. The expression "Use it or lose it" really applies to the brain. Neuronal pathways that are not used simply die off.

There are some central issues in every society that constantly communicate ideas that are not our own. We are bombarded with the drumbeat of media messages about politics, violence, money, religion, sports. weather, etc. I am worried that they are shaping our neuronal pathways toward things of less and less importance.

The result is that the plastic nature of the brain shapes itself to these constant reiterations and everybody thinks they have the correct attitudes toward politics, money and religion, etc. There is no need to try to convince people to change. You cannot change with reason any attitude that was not formed by reason.

On the positive side, plasticity offers the chance to change. We need to challenge our comfort zones, to learn, to experiment with newness and freshness, to engage our brain. And there is a world of knowledge waiting for us to assimilate and expand our understanding. It is the path to growth. The only difference between being in a rut and a grave is a matter of depth.

We live in an age of explosive new learning. Our understanding of almost everything is expanding exponentially. I do not think that living with a static theological creed serves us well. Therefore, I choose to remain open to the newness of life and to hold my beliefs tentatively, always willing to change with new, tested and confirmed information. Life is dynamic and a static belief system is destined to be obsolete in a world that is forever changing.

As a child, I remember going to the movie every Saturday morning to see the next exciting episode of one of those serialized Western films. I could hardly wait to see what would happen next. Today, as an adult, I have very much the same feeling of wonder and excitement about what they will learn next about the brain. Waiting and watching this real-life drama makes life very interesting for me and, no doubt, very disturbing to others with preconceived opinions.

Contribution to Civilization

The histories of the Christian Church and of Western Civilization were closely related for many centuries. As time moved on, however, a distinct cultural and secular movement emerged in parallel with the Church. This move out of the Middle Ages was called the Renaissance and dates from the 12th to the 17th Centuries. It was characterized by a loss of awe for the state of affairs, a revival of the classics and a conviction that modern man had as much to contribute to Civilization as did the Greeks and Romans.

An outgrowth of the Renaissance was an initiative called natural philosophy (known today as science) that tried to explain the mechanics of life by a new technique known as experimentation. Beyond 1620 Western Civilization was much more than church history. There was a split that competed for the path to truth: intuition and experimentation. I thought an interesting way to present history beyond this point was to contrast the relative contributions to society of the church and the secular world.

The early church had an aura of respectability, even though there were periods of despicable governance in the Papacy. The Church commanded allegiance out of love of the faith and the fear to question it. So much so that city after city competed with each other around the 12th Century to build the finest cathedrals that we marvel at today. They developed architectural methods – often by trial and costly error – that exceeded anything ever known before. They became patrons of the artists that produced unparalleled paintings, statuary, music and stained glass of exquisite beauty. The scribes working in various monasteries hand-copied manuscripts to serve the needs for teaching and preserving the heritage. And the monks made contributions to early agriculture with new gardening techniques. Of great significance, Mendel did creative work in heredity and genes (although on his own time). There is no doubt that the Church's contributions brought beauty and inspiration to civilization. And it can be argued that these are the things that civilization needs most.

The church has kept the flames of hope alive for millions of people who suffer. Hope is a subtle and delicate thing. But when the spirits of people are depressed, it is hope that keeps them alive. We see this over and over in culture after culture. When people are in pain due to anything – the economy, illness, storms, crisis – they turn to a hope that is more spiritual than luck.

In addition, there have been many individuals who have been inspired by religion and have gone on to make great contributions to society. I think of Abraham Lincoln, Martin Luther King, Jr. and Mother Theresa. But it is only fair to give the credit to the individuals who make the effort and took the risk, not to the church.

When I started itemizing the relative contributions, the more I felt this was unfair to the church. One could argue that it was not the function of the church to contribute to the improvement of society. But that is a weak argument. The church had the manpower and wealth to do whatever it wished. It simply did not have the desire to understand the world in a way that would challenge its theology. Nor did the church struggle to improve the lives of ordinary people by making them more healthy, happy or comfortable. I see little evidence of a vision to enhance society as a whole. However, they did very well by their own aggrandizement.

On the other hand, the goal of the secular efforts has been to understand the nature of the real world. It had the advantage of not being encumbered by doctrine. It was a search for truth that could be found only in nature. And from this new found knowledge, we have seen the outpouring of an enormous number of inventions that has led to tools, instruments, machinery, health-care products, communication, transportation, etc., that has significantly improved the quality of life for most people.

The contributions of science and the secular world are more

generally tangible. It is very easy to list the great contributions that advanced civilization. Names like Copernicus, Bacon, Vesalius, Harvey, Tycho, Kepler, Gilbert, Galileo, Newton, Faraday and on and on come to mind for starters without getting into modern times. But one cannot omit the all-time greatest contributors with the deepest insights of all time, those of Copernicus, Newton, Darwin, Einstein and Crick.

For over four centuries, science has progressively tried to understand these laws of nature.. As Timothy Ferris says in *The Science of Liberty*, "The scientific revolution is still gathering momentum, but has already revealed more about the universe than had been learned in all prior history, while technological applications of scientific knowledge has rescued billions from poverty, ignorance, fear, and an early grave." And science has done these things without an ideology, without a creed, without conscription and without wars. It advances not by authority or revelation, but by exploring the wonders and mysteries of life by the disciplined and objective search for truth using experimentation.

More often than not the Christian Church is known for opposing ideas that conflicted with its world-view. Rather than contributing to civilization, it has frequently opposed the advances of science and medicine. Moreover, in the defense of its doctrine, it has engaged in wars, crusades and Inquisitions that have left it with the blood of many innocent people on its hands.

The low point for the Christian Church and the high point for pure reason was the Enlightenment. Philosophers tried to use the methods of science and apply them to social systems. They addressed questions like what was the best form of government, education, finance and penal reform. From this secular effort we got the great contributions of Montesquieu, Adams, Rousseau, Voltaire, Diderot, D'Alembert, and Beccaria. It was Montesquieu's famous *Spirit of the Laws* that proposed three separate governmental bodies --legislative, executive and judicial --to achieve the separation of powers that was adopted in the US Constitution. And closer to home, my mother – who Americanized her name to Madge – was influenced by Rousseau's book, *Emile*, on raising children and gave me a lot of rope to explore my small world as a child.

Of course, most of these ideas were reactions to the excesses of power and control of the times by both the monarchies and the church and especially to the "marriage" of the two. Naturally, large social systems did not lend themselves to experimentation. But when the tensions get very high, they often lead to revolutions. And the Enlightenment did lead to the French Revolution. The feeling of the times was expressed by Baron Paul d'Holbach in 1761 in his book *Christianity Unveiled*, a frontal assault upon the alliance of Church and state, which anticipated Marx's description of religion as the "opium of the people."

"Religion is the art of intoxicating men with enthusiasm [the eighteenth century term for religious fervor] to prevent them from dealing with the evils with which their governors oppress them…The art of reigning has become nothing more than that of profiting from the errors and abjection of mind and soul into which superstition has plunged the nations…By means of threatening men with invisible powers, they [Church and state] force them to suffer in silence the miseries with which visible powers afflict them. They are made to hope that if they agree to being unhappy in this world, they will be happy in the next…Instead of morality the Christian is taught the miraculous fables and inconceivable dogmas of a religion thoroughly hostile to right reason. From his very first step in his studies he is taught to distrust the evidence of his senses, to subdue his reason... and to rely blindly on the authority of his master…Those who have shaken themselves free from these notions find themselves powerless against errors sucked in with their mother's milk."

The more that the champions of the Enlightenment studied these issues, the more they realized that the church and the state were in bed with each other for their own advantage. This led to the overthrow of the government in the French Revolution and the shutting down of the Catholic Church in France for a number of years. Citizens were so mad that they changed the unit of measure from feet (the length of the King's foot) to the metric system. They changed the names of the days and the months that contained reference to state or church heroes. The Catholic Church was not re-admitted to France until 1801 when Napoleon authorized its return as a sop to the peasants.

What we have witnessed is that new ideas stimulate other ideas. Knowledge that is shared builds on itself. As a result, science has flourished and mankind has benefitted. A closed system does not grow while an open system expands exponentially. If I drew a hypothetical graph of the relative contributions of the sacred and secular worlds to society, the church contributions would be a line slowly sloping up from the x-axis and the secular contributions wound be an exponential curve starting in 1600 and skyrocketing into outer space. And the difference is only in the methodology for pursuing truth.

This contrast leaves me no option but to align myself with the power of science with its instrumentation and un-biased pursuit of truth wherever it leads. I stand with an open, non-doctrinal system, embracing experimentation, evidence and confirmation as the best path to truth, however tentative.

Part III

Uncoupling with Grace

The End of One Road

Above all, I hope I have been fair to my readers and myself in the foregoing analysis. It is a profoundly serious subject for me. And it took a very long time to free myself from the mythology of my past.

But the sum of my takeaway thoughts doesn't leave much wiggle room. I have rejected these things: (1) a capital-G God, (2) a Jesus as being divine, (3) a theology that was hammered out in debate and acrimony and enforced by the powers of the state, (4) religion claiming morality and spirituality, (5) the ability to fulfill the basic bargain, (6) the top-down approaches to truth, (7) thinking one's way to cosmic conclusions, (8) earth as the center of the universe, (9) supernaturalism, (10) creationism, (10) man's dominion over all, (11) being made in the image of God, (12) that intangible things are beyond science, (13) the value of fixed beliefs, and (14) the idea that the church has significantly benefited society.

Specifically, I realize I cannot believe in the dogma of the Christian church or any other creedal religion. Nor can I accept things on faith. So many atrocities have been done in the name of faith. I feel sure that the Nazis of Germany, the Communists of Russia and the religious terrorists of Islam all had enormous faith in their endeavors.

Let me be specific.

I believe that the universe if far too complex for the human to comprehend at this time. I am willing to call all the things I do not understand mysteries and live with the uncertainty.

I believe all mystery will turn out to be natural when understood and therefore I do not think of mystery in religious terms as divine, miraculous or godly, but simply as unresolved issues of nature. We are not smart enough yet, by half.

I do not believe in a personal god.

I do not believe in life after death.

I do not believe that a life is judged to spend an eternity in heaven or hell.

I do not pray, although I acknowledge that prayers have value to the one who prays and maybe to the recipient of prayers. I just can't believe prayers are routed through a god for action.

I do not think that man has a soul apart from the body, but is a manifestation of our immensely complex electro-chemical systems.

I view every living creature as a miracle.

I do not believe that revelation is sealed. Rather we have a personal responsibility to seek new insights, to find new truths, and to progressively refine old truths. I believe that doubt is a virtue and a friend of the truth.

I do not believe that God has anything to do with personal religion, only institutional religions. Personal religion is entirely an internal struggle to come to grips with your life. It is overcoming fear and greed and replacing them with courage and generosity. It is building community on a one-by-one basis, not by group think. It is finding abundance in all the landscapes of your life and dwelling in trust and love.

I do not believe that there is a grand purpose in life into which I was born to fill some role. Whatever purposes arise are distilled from engaging life and they change dynamically as our experiences change and we commit ourselves to new endeavors.

I do not believe that there is a grand meaning in life. I have a T-shirt that says it all: "The meaning of life is to give life meaning." Meaning is a dynamic crystallizing of experiences and changes as we grow with involvement. Meaning emerges from rising to the challenge and knowing you can make a difference, whether it is in parenting a child, doing a job well, or helping others. Meaning comes from finding ways to involve the self where there are needs.

I think that the church continues to do a good job in building community. It meets the needs of people to congregate, socialize and validate each other's lives.

I have simply come to believe that no religion can live up to its part of the bargain of providing an after-life. Yet it continues to teach an out-dated theology and breed false hopes. It has become an enormous business selling hope and, in many ways, detracting attention and resources from the true problems and suffering in the world.

I regret having to dissociate myself from the tenets of Christian theology that are so meaningful to most of my relatives and friends. I am not just uncoupling from Christianity, but from all creedal religions. This in no way implies that I am parting from my relatives and friends. They are among the most important parts of my life. It simply means we will have differences in theology, but not in love and respect.

This is not done in a mean-spirited way. It results from much study, much analysis, and a need to follow the integrity of my own thoughts.

I do believe I am part of a system of natural laws along with all animal and plant life. I see myself as a humanist. I am of this world only. And I will try to stand in right relationship with all people regardless of their beliefs.

I hope they will treat me as gently.

The Road Less Travelled

It is the business of the future to be dangerous…
The major advances in civilization are processes that
all but wreck the societies in which they occur.
Alfred North Whitehead

I mentioned at the beginning that uncoupling from mystical religion only returns us to ground zero. We are where we started before becoming indoctrinated with the beliefs of others. But we can't drive in neutral and life demands that we go forward. Someone said that you can stand still, balanced on a bicycle, but that is not what bicycles are made for. So let's try to think through this.

The world has become too small, the technology too advanced, the weapons too powerful, the politics too extreme, the religions too intransient and the rhetoric too loud. We live in a world of increasing diversity that challenges the security that our ancestral world provided.

We need to find something that we can agree upon to unify our fractured civilization. Certainly it would not be our religions, our politics or our philosophies. These "top-down" concepts are the arbitrary things that divide us. As lofty as they sound, they have been the historic sources of many of our problems, including biases, hatred, violence, and war. I respect that they are all trying to answer cosmic questions of personal consequence. But dreamed-up, arbitrary and un-tested answers will no longer do, however comforting.

For me, the issue is bigger than religion, politics or philosophy. The issue is humanity itself and our ability to survive collectively and peacefully.

What, then, do we have to build on? What is universal and everyone agrees with?

First, I made the case that experimentation is the only approach to truth that all people universally agreed with. That's a very good start. So we have a methodology for reaching future truths that people will accept.

Secondly, natural laws are universally accepted as being consistent, dependable and impartial. That is an undeniable truth and strength we can depend on.

Third, the functioning of DNA in our lives has proven its utility through eons of time by adapting to our needs and is favorable and beneficial to our survival.

Think about it. Recall that there are three fundamental DNA strategies governing life: adaptation to the environment, survival and reproduction. It is beyond question that these fundamental "rules" support life. Our genes have survived for millions of years, being passed from generation to generation in an unbroken line. They have passed the test of time. And it is just possible that they could be the basis of rules for the survival of society as well as the basis for the survival of individuals.

By DNA, I do not simply mean just the chemical molecule of our genetics. I emphatically mean the information it contains and its awesome ability to progressively develop a human out of chemicals with unbelievably complex organisms like the brain, lungs and liver with rules for regulating, rebuilding and repairing itself.

Starting with the microscopically small sperm and egg, this self-contained coded intelligence produces a god-like miracle of manifesting full-blown life with not only complex organs but ephemeral qualities like consciousness and feelings. The DNA wants us to survive and to help others to survive. To this end, it evolved mirror neurons so that we can feel the pain of others in distress and hopefully help.

Your DNA cares for you more than anything else in your life. Unlike natural laws that are impartial, your DNA is dedicated uniquely to you 24/7. What else in life even comes close to being ever present for your advantage. In Sunday school I was told that God watches over me and knows every hair on my head. I didn't believe it. But your DNA does exactly that and more.

It is a very small step to consider the DNA's strategy and its logical extensions as a basis for human morality. Above all things, the DNA wants us to survive so we can reproduce, adjust to the environment and keep the game moving forward, not just for some of us but for all of us. The DNA is already universal and serves humanity.

So I think it is fair and logical to conclude that a moral code that conforms and supports the genetic code is simply this: **Do no harm to others, help them when needed, and adapt to new knowledge.** This is not very different from the Golden Rule that appeared in all cultures simultaneously when we started living in larger groups and the DNA started adapting genetically to this new environment. This is an awesome realization.

The last step is to add to this genetically based moral code only additions that conform to natural law and truths that were confirmed by experimentation. This would guarantee universal acceptance. If this simple moral code did prevail, it would argue against wars, murder, social injustice of all kinds and violence. How simple.

If it were possible to have a moral code based on the genetic code, it would have a number of advantages. First, it would be common to all people of all nationalities, genders, creeds, eras, and political persuasions. Second, it would not have to be taught; it would be inherent. And third, there should be fewer violations of the code. It is when arbitrary "rules" are enforced that are inconsistent with the genetic-moral code that violence increases.

Somehow this seems too simple. In a world of complex rules and regulations, it is hard to imagine going back to such a simple concept of morality. But any thoughtful expansion of this basic moral proposition of gene survival removes a lot of artificiality and supports the logic of live and let live.

We have seen this moral of basic survival work remarkably on our highways. It always amazes me that millions of cars driving at high speeds so close to each other and having no communications between them have relatively so few accidents. Yes, they break the speed limits; yes, they cut in front of others; yes they turn without signaling. They break many of societies' rules of the road, but they honor the moral of survival.

By contrast, think about culturally prescribed "moral" laws. Many are quite arbitrary. Others change as social mores change like in the Victorian Era. We have seen that utopian ideals presented as rules for social conduct fail time and time again. The Communist egalitarian goal of having each give according to his ability and receive according to his needs failed because it denied the genetic drive for a meaningful survival. The Roman Catholic Church's requirement of celibacy among priest since 1058 C.E. denies the strong genetic drive for reproduction and has had limited and questionable success.

Utopian rules breed hypocrisy. People naturally want to appear to conform to social mores, but more deeply they want to follow their genetic drives. So we breed a society that often says one thing and does another. Such utopian rules violate the most basic chemistry underlying human behavior.

This much seems certain: any arbitrary moral code that is counter to the genetic code is destined to fail. Life is not arbitrary and the moral rules regulating life should not be arbitrary. Rather, morality should sustain, enhance and support the genetic rules of life itself.

I have written elsewhere that I believe that we have an internal moral code – each and every one of us, universally the same – that is based on our genetic code. It is an extension of the gene's need for survival by not harming others. We don't need the Ten Commandments to tell us not to kill, hurt, steal or take advantage of others. We know this in our guts. The DNA put it there. And by "our," I mean every single living person of every age who is mentally sane.

This truth is universal and could be unifying when we come to live by it. But how? Currently, there are so many partisan belief systems – religious, political, economic and philosophical – that separate us in the interest of sustaining their institutions. Maybe it is time for the inter-faith councils of many religions to champion this. Or maybe an international body like the United Nations should advocate it like they did in promoting the Declaration of Human Rights.

Until that "miracle" happens, and without belief in god or a creedal religion, I will steer my life by a few simple principles that conform to a genetic based moral code.

Man is a social animal. The greatest human need is for acceptance and the greatest human fear is rejection. Each of us needs to have his or her life confirmed. We no longer live in a tribal community of uniformity. We live in an increasingly complex world of rich diversity. It is my world and I want to enjoy and celebrate the diversity. Therefore the most fundamental ethic for relating to others is to be genuinely accepting and help others feel good about themselves, to avoid being judgmental, critical and rejecting, to be positively and unconditionally accepting of one another regardless of gender, race, color, or creed. I try to engage the inner person. I try to meet people constructively where they are and learn from them. I may not succeed, but I know what is right.

I cherish the pursuit of truth. I thrill to the excitement of exploration, of questioning, of learning. Because of this, I cannot accept any thesis – social, political or religious – that claims to have the final truth. For me, that ranks with the highest level of arrogance and a total lack of humility. Neither can I respect anyone who has given up the excitement of the search for the comfort of an imagined truth. I firmly agree with Emerson that, "Nothing is at last sacred except the integrity of your own mind." The ultimate dishonesty is lying to one's self.

I believe that the personal spiritual journey consists of coming to accept yourself, recognizing that all the real battles are fought within the self, and true growth and happiness come from transcending the ego and freeing one's self from negative feelings.

I believe in serving causes greater than self. I believe in engaging the world, being helpful, and trying to make a positive difference. I believe I should participate generously and constructively in the needs of the community, to help where I can make a difference, to keep learning and to teach when it is appropriate, to be regarded as truthful and responsible, to make and retain friends, to be true to my core convictions and to seek ever higher values to emulate.

I believe that society will be better and safer in proportion to the number of people who succeed in the spiritual work of transcending their egos and working for the betterment of the community.

I believe that the highest values are those that affect the most people. These are the values that instill certainty, security and comfort, namely truth, justice and love.

I believe that selfishness is a natural behavior and generosity has to be learned and reinforced. But we know that the world is a better place where generosity prevails. Therefore, I try to be generous with my time, my ideas, my help and my resources. It would please me to think I have made a difference in someone's life and I will leave the world a better place than I inherited.

I know that gratitude is the parent of generosity. I have been blessed in life in many ways and I am very grateful. The word that characterizes my life is abundance, not scarcity. I want to share my good fortune to help others feel gratitude, in the hope it will birth even more generosity.

My time on this earth is limited. I do not intend to waste it in the hope of a future life. If I am wrong, I win twice. Therefore, I am a doer. I get involved. I invest myself in many causes that complement my values. I enjoy the challenge whether it be studying, inventing, writing, constructing, teaching or playing music. I thrive on seeing something done well, whether it is someone else's art or architecture, or my own modest achievements. I really don't like idle time, except for that all-important centering process for integrating ideas into meaningful wholes.

Best of all, I believe the rational, scientific approach I have enumerated here allows me to retain my integrity. I am not hesitant to say, "I could be wrong." On the other hand, no creedal religion I know dares to say it could be wrong, although there are numerous conflicting creedal religions. And the members of creedal religions I know do not seem to be free to say, "I could be wrong."

I hope this adds up to: **Do no harm to others, help them when needed, and adapt to new knowledge.**

When a friend, Martha Atherton, saw my title, *From God to DNA*, she was quick to remind me that when people are suffering, they pray to God, not to their DNA. I well understand this. But I see it as a misplaced, habitual reaction. In today's world, when I become sick and need help, I would much prefer to place my confidence in the information coded in my DNA than to wait for help from the historical God of my local culture.

Mea Culpa. I realize that this provocative journey is an example of top-down thinking. A life's journey does not lend itself to experimentation and can only be understood in hindsight. But this is not a frivolous bit of top-down thinking. It is based on serious historical studies, exacting scientific experimentation, and blended together with a genuine concern for where knowledge is leading us and where I want to be. I have no desire to be the last man applauding yesterday's parade after it has passed.

END
RRS/rrs

Bio of Rembert "Rem" Stokes

The author received a BS in mechanical engineering from Clemson University and a MS is Educational Psychology from Butler University. He worked for Bell Telephone Laboratories for 25 years designing telephone apparatus. Following the divestiture of the Bell System, he worked for Motorola as an engineering manager until his retirement in 1994. He holds 22 patents and is the inventor of the laminated coinage used by the U.S. Treasury since 1964 to save the cost of silver. His first book is entitled *Systematic Approach to Problem Solving.* He taught Design of Experiments at Motorola University and, after retirement, history and investments at the Institute for Continued Learning at Roosevelt University. Throughout his adult life he has made a "Ministry of Money" by helping churches on 77 occasions with financial issues. His second book is entitled *Cultivating Generosity: Giving What's Right, Not What's Left.*

This current book explores his transition from the mystical religion of his youth to a profoundly different understanding of human nature, coupled with an appreciation for the advancements of science and especially neuroscience. He is married and lives in Barrington, Illinois.

www.ingramcontent.com/pod-product-compliance
Ingram Content Group UK Ltd.
Pitfield, Milton Keynes, MK11 3LW, UK
UKHW041941190726
13854UKWH00004B/1722